DELI SARKIS:
THE SCARS
HE CARRIED

For Marge
In remembrance of all
who died unseen,
neither sanctified
or honored.
Rest in Peace.
Ellen Sarkisian Chesnut

DELI SARKIS:
THE SCARS
HE CARRIED

Ellen Sarkisian Chesnut

Two Harbors Press
322 First Avenue N, 5th floor
Minneapolis, MN 55401
612.455.2293
www.TwoHarborsPress.com

ISBN-13: 978-1-62652-916-8
LCCN: 2014910716

Distributed by Itasca Books

Cover: Sarkis in the Greek army in Bursa, Turkey, 1921.
Back cover: A small leather passport and important document case used by Sarkis. Dikran Nahabedian, Sarkis (in center seated), and Antranik Minassian (standing on right) in Sophia, Bulgaria, 1924. Wedding picture of Evelyn and Sarkis in Mosul, Iraq, July 3, 1938. A Kurdish man, Sarkis on a donkey while Yegisheh stands alongside in Mosul, Iraq, 1938.

Set in: Bembo and Frutiger.

Printed in the United States of America

This book is dedicated to my siblings:
Arthur Minas (1940–2007) and
Janet Anahid (1943–2013). You were the
playmates of my childhood and my friends
in later years and you will live forever in
my heart. To my husband, Glen, for your
encouragement and support while I toiled
through the research and writing of this
book. For my father, Sarkis Deli Sarkisian,
and my mother, Evelyn, who both survived
the Armenian Genocide of 1915–1923.
Finally, to all of the people who lived,
loved, and toiled in the Armenian village
of Keramet in the Southern Marmara
region of Turkey. You will never be forgotten.

TABLE OF CONTENTS

The first step in liquidating a people is to erase its memory. Destroy its books, its culture, its history. Then you have somebody write new books, manufacture a new culture, invent a new history. Before long the nation will begin to forget what it is and what it was.

Milan Kundera,
The Book of Laughter and Forgetting

EUREKA VALLEY LIBRARY, SAN FRANCISCO, 1953. I'm in the lower ninth grade at Everett Junior High School in Robert Sturtevant's social studies class and doing research for a paper on my ancestral people, the Armenians. I look through one set of encyclopedias after another getting increasingly frustrated. Something is very wrong as there are just miniscule references in the encyclopedias and very little in the history books of any relevance to my report. It's almost as if the Armenians do not exist, and what my parents told me of our proud history is a fantasy in their own minds.

My mother, Evelyn (born 1910), who was from Marash, Turkey, spoke of the ruins of fortresses and castles that dotted the landscape south of her city, evidence of the once great Armenian kingdom of Cilicia. My father spoke of the sparkling waters of Iznik Lake near his village of Keramet teeming with fish, and before the lake appeared, in prehistoric times, the once-glorious city of copper.

The Armenians are an Indo-European people who have lived in the area of Turkey for close to three thousand years. Originally they were a tribal people who, with other Indo-Europeans, flooded the tablelands of eastern Anatolia or Asia Minor (between the Black and the Mediterranean seas) in about the seventh century before Christ.

Armenians contributed mightily to the Byzantine Empire, supplying it with emperors, religious leaders, intellectuals, diplomats, and generals. When the Byzantine Empire collapsed in 1453, and the Ottoman Turks took over, Armenians were conscripted into the service of the empire and were engaged in all aspects of Ottoman society. That is, until all Armenians living in the Ottoman Empire were forcibly removed during the First World War.

In the nineteenth century, still under Ottoman rule, periodic massacres targeting the Armenians began. According to my mother's father, Hagop Shamlian (1866–1960), and her grandfather Toros Shamlian (1840–1904), Armenians were subjected to these atrocities every twenty years or so but would repair their destroyed homes and businesses and start anew.

The Hamidian massacres were far worse. Between the years 1894–1896, in a very wide region of Turkey close to 250,000 Armenians were butchered.

Many women and children were forcibly taken and Islamized, while over 500,000 others were left destitute and homeless. Sultan Abdul Hamid II sanctioned the killings. Another massacre took place in 1909. Twenty-five thousand Armenians were slaughtered including itinerant laborers. A group of rabid Turkish nationalists known as the Young Turks played a role in instigating this massacre. It happened in the area of Adana and included my mother's city of Marash.

The Young Turks took over the government in 1908, overthrowing the sultan, and became known as the Committee of Union and Progress (CUP). Under the leadership of Mehmet Talaat, the minister of the interior, Ismail Enver, the minister of war, and Ahmed Cemal, the minister of the navy, the CUP wanted to get rid of the Armenians once and for all for political, economic, cultural, and religious reasons. Under cover of the First World War they moved ahead.

THE FINAL SOLUTION. On April 24, 1915, over 250 Armenian leaders were arrested in Istanbul and other regions of Turkey. These men had distinguished themselves in all areas of Turkish society: religious, literary, civil, commercial, and artistic. After the arrests they were transported to outlying areas and murdered. The next step was the arrests of able-bodied men and boys who were taken out of their towns and villages and killed. Finally women, children, and the elderly were given two or three days to close up their homes, take whatever they could carry, and, under guard, walk to the deserts of Syria and Mesopotamia (Iraq). Women, girls, and boys were forcibly snatched away from their families, never to be seen again. The rest struggled without food or water until their suffering was relieved by death. One and a half million Armenians died during the years 1915–1923 as a direct result of the genocidal practices of the Young Turk regime.

Beginning with the creation of the Turkish Republic in 1923, successive governments in Turkey, including the government in power now, have denied the reality of the genocide. This conveniently absolves the perpetrators of their crimes against humanity. There is an official document in the Turkish archives that was signed by Talaat on May 27, 1915, known as the Tehcir Law that is proof of the genocidal intent of the Young Turks. In

Turkish, *tehcir* means deportation, and the official name of the document is *Sevk ve Iskan Kanunu* (Dispatchment and Settlement Law).

In 1915 the *Valis* (regional governors) in all of the villages and towns populated by Armenians had statistics of property owned by those who would disappear. When the Armenians were gone from their ancestral homeland, their property was distributed to the Turkish citizenry at a fraction of its value.

I believe that the great-grandparents of the people now living in Turkey spoke about what had happened: some perhaps even bragged about how they raped and killed with no remorse. I'm also sure that they have in their homes items that had been in the possession of their murdered victims: jewelry, cookware, bedding, and beautiful lacework. Most precious of all were the tens of thousands of our parentless children who were forcibly taken by gendarmes, Turkish or Kurdish villagers, or government officials for their own use or were placed in Turkish orphanages, i.e., Turkification centers. Their Armenian names were changed to Turkish ones, and the boys, some as young as three, four, and five years of age, were circumcised to conform to Muslim practices.

Fethiye Cetin, a Turkish human-rights lawyer, tells of discovering that her grandmother Seher (Armenian name Heranus) was one of those children forcibly taken in 1915 by a Turkish gendarme captain and adopted by him. Her story is in her memoir, *My Grandmother*.

PUTTING THE PIECES TOGETHER, 1988. My father was living by himself in San Francisco in the Victorian flat that he had owned with my mother, Evelyn. She died on January 29, 1983, of heart failure. We believed him when he said he could take care of himself. One day in 1988 my youngest sister, Lucy, arrived to take him for his hearing appointment. She discovered him. He was face up, unconscious. She called the fire department and he was immediately rushed to the emergency ward of San Francisco General Hospital. The doctor asked me if there was something wrong with my father mentally, as he could not communicate. It turned out he had bronchial pneumonia and a brain concussion. After he had spent some time in a convalescent facility to gain his strength, my sister Lucy found a group home for him on Forty-Eighth Avenue in San Francisco. He would be living with a small group of other seniors. The place was Kelly Home, and a young couple, Mark and Candy Myers, took care of the cooking and care of the residents. My father so enjoyed it there, as he was with people when he needed company and could be alone when he craved silence.

I knew then that I needed to speak to him about his story and that of his village of Keramet, because if he died it would all be gone. Every time I visited him I asked him questions about his life and took notes. All the interviews resulted in my writing down his memoirs. I read aloud what I had written and he approved and signed his name. This was our routine from 1988 until his death in 1995. At the same time I wrote letters to Armenian newspapers in the United States and in France and also to the Armenian Church in Sophia, Bulgaria, looking for people from Keramet. Nazareth Bidanian, a local scholar, wrote letters in Armenian for me to mail overseas, and when I received replies he translated them into English.

Louisa Boghosian and Siranoush Todoravna, who were living in Bulgaria and were the daughters of Yezekel Garabed Ashirian (my father's best friend from his childhood days), wrote back. They learned that someone from San Francisco was inquiring about their father. They hoped I was their father's long-lost sister Siranoush, who had been taken in Syria during the deportations. Included with their letter was a photograph of their father taken in 1986. Sadly, he had already died when the letter was sent.

In America, I heard from Stephan Karadian of West Bloomfield, Michigan, whose father, Sahag, was from Soloz, across the lake from Keramet. Soloz was the birthplace of the famous Armenian writer Hagop Oshagan.

Stephan had read my inquiry in the *Armenian Weekly* newspaper and gave me the phone number of Varsenig Topouzian, who was from Cengiler, a village near Keramet. She was living at the Saint Sarkis Seniors Home in Detroit, Michigan. Luckily for me, Varsenig's sister-in-law, Florence Pashayan, was visiting her at the time and learned of my inquiry. Florence's mother, Aghavni, was from Keramet.

With Florence's help I was able to correspond with her relatives in France, who also had a connection to the village, as Florence's mother's first cousin Hagop Nigogossian was born there. In 1990 I received the memoirs of Hagop Nigogossian. His daughter Shakeh Samouelian sent this valuable link to my father's story, and I have included an excerpt from his memoirs in chapter seven of this book. Credit must also be given to the daughter of my father's first cousin, Suzanne Bakalian, who was also living in France. She sent me invaluable statistics compiled and completed in 1966 in Bourgas, Bulgaria, by Garabed Papazian, a former resident of the village. My father had corresponded regularly with Garabed in the 1950s and 1960s. They shared information about their village. In 1992, I took the memoirs of Hagop to Nazareth Bidanian, and he transcribed the cursive of the memoirs to a more readable text on his Armenian keyed typewriter. In three weeks he had completed the typing of the manuscript. Upon completion he sat down with me and read aloud chapters about Keramet that not only showed the bravery of villagers but also the heartrending trials that they were subjected to, and that's why they are in this book.

A word or two about Nazareth, who was the most self-effacing man you could ever meet: His education began in an elementary school in Musa Dagh, Turkey. He went to secondary school at the Antilias seminary in Lebanon and always had a love for literature. After he graduated from the French College in Antioch, Turkey, Nazareth taught Armenian literature and math to high school students in Lebanon for twenty-five years.

On September 7, 1946, in Lebanon, Nazareth married Sosse Shrikian, the daughter of a priest. On June 13, 1947, Nazareth survived a horrible automobile accident on the road from Anjar to Baalbek, Lebanon. Four people died. Nazareth survived but was severely burned, spending eighteen months in a hospital where a thumb was made for his right hand while his remaining fingers were just stubs. That didn't stop him from typing sixty words per minute. I feel very fortunate that Nazareth worked with me while doing research for this book, for without his help the book would not be as complete.

In 2010, I took the memoirs of Hagop Nigogossian to Archdeacon Sevag Badoyan of Saint Gregory Armenian Apostolic Church in San Francisco, and working together we translated into English the information found in chapter seven of this book.

Brass Bowl with enamel inlay, 4.5 inches in circumference.
It was purchased by Evelyn and Sarkis in Bombay, India, 1941.
"Made in British India" is inscribed on the bottom.

CHAPTER 1

TURKEY,
THEN AND NOW

Keramet, Turkey, June 2009. Newer buildings and pink paving stones. What remains intact of the Armenians who were once the majority population of this lovely village are the rolling hills, the abundant orchards of olive trees that they cared for after they returned from the deportations, and their fond memories.

JUNE 3, 2009. Hotel Savoy in Taksim Square, Istanbul, Turkey. It's been quite a trip so far visiting the ancestral sites of Cilician Armenia. I had arranged beforehand for our tour guide, Armen Aroyan, the founder of the Armenian Heritage Society, to take me to my father's village of Keramet in the Southern Marmara region of Turkey. These past weeks of touring, organized by the National Association of Armenian Studies and Research, under the guidance and expertise of Dr. Richard R. Hovannisian and Armen Aroyan, opened my eyes to the almost total destruction of our cultural heritage.

I saw the town of Kirikhan, now in Turkey, but in the 1920s it belonged to Syria. My mother, Evelyn, and her sister Rebecca, newly minted graduates of the American Girls High School in Aleppo, taught school in Armenian villages in northern Syria. They attended Sunday services in the small Armenian Church of Saint Gregory the Illuminator in Kirikhan. When they were there in the late 1920s it was a lovely church filled with worshippers. What I saw in 2009 was something totally different: nothing but stone walls with dirt and rocks littering the ground, as if the building had been pulverized to its foundation.

As I waited for Armen and the cab that would take us to the ferry terminal, I thought back to my previous trip to Turkey in the summer of 1970. At that time Istanbul had a vibrant Armenian community of over eighty thousand souls. There were thirty-five Armenian churches, and Archbishop Shnork Kalousdian was the patriarch of the Armenians of Turkey. My brother Arthur had raved about his trip to Europe in 1965 and his visits with my father's relatives in France. That's why I wanted to go, too. I would start my adventure in England because in 1970, the University of California at Berkeley launched its first summer study program in conjunction with Worcester College in Oxford. I loved art so I enrolled in History of British Painting, taught by Kenneth Garlick, keeper of Western art at the Ashmolean Museum. While the trip was still in its planning stages, my dream of riding the Orient Express to Bulgaria and then on to Istanbul was derailed. My father received a letter from Bulgaria informing him that his relatives were too upset to take me in as a visitor because one of their young men had run off with a much older woman. So instead of taking the train I would go to France and then fly into Istanbul when my class ended. The class at Worcester College took up half of each day. The other half was for sightseeing and doing homework. On weekends I'd travel to London, by train, to go to the museums and the theater. One weekend, I stayed at the Rembrandt Hotel in room 556. It was a very elegant place, and my room had an enormous window opening to the awesome sight of the Victoria and Albert Museum across the street.

I went to the British Museum, the National Gallery, and John Soane's Museum. I saw the play *Heloise and Abelard* starring Diana Rigg and Keith Michell at the Wyndham Theatre, Charing Cross Road. I saw *Sleuth* starring Anthony Quayle and Keith Baxter at Saint Martin's Theatre on West Street in London. In Stratford-upon-Avon, I saw *Richard III* with Norman Rodway as Richard and the young Helen Mirren as Lady Ann. Back in Oxford, I saw the Royal Ballet performing *Swan Lake* at the New Theatre.

When my summer class ended, it was off to Dover, where I went aboard the Hovercraft that took me to Boulogne, France. In 1970, taking the Hovercraft was the way to cross the channel. I stayed at the Hotel du Square Monge in Paris. The sights and sounds of Paris and its environs were wonderful. But I especially enjoyed my trip to Chartres. It was there that I met a Japanese tourist, about as young as I was, who indicated that he would like to travel with me. Neither one of us could speak a word of French, but between the two of us I'm sure we would have managed and would have enjoyed ourselves. I'm sorry to this day that I didn't accept his offer, as my time in France would have been a much happier experience if it had been shared with another person. I found the people there at the time to be rather unfriendly and cold. I can say the same thing for my father's relatives in France. Looking back, I realize that one cannot know the troubles people are going through in their personal lives, so I do not want to be harsh in my judgments.

On July 27, 1970, I traveled via Air France to Istanbul, as I would be staying with my father's second cousin Egsapet Baharyan. My father and mother had arranged it. The Istanbul airport was smaller then and definitely not the busy place it would become in 2009. Happily, I did not have to look too far as I saw a group of six dark-eyed people staring at me. I guessed that they were my father's relatives.

They came over to me with warm greetings that I understood because my mother and father spoke both Armenian and Turkish. Sadly, my parents did not insist that we children converse with them in their native languages at home, because they wanted so much for us to assimilate. This has been a great loss for me, as I'm sure I too would have become a fluent speaker.

Egsapet kissed me on both cheeks. I liked her right away. She was a short, stout, blue-eyed woman and as light as a feather on her feet. She also had a twinkle in her eye and a very confident and no-nonsense demeanor. I knew we would get along. She was the mother of seven sons, three of whom were deceased. One of her sons, Hovannes, still lived at home. Everybody called him Onnik. He was learning to be a jeweler and eventually would become a master designer. He was in his twenties and engaged to be married. His fiancée was Shahaniki, nineteen years old, slender, dark haired and the only girl in a family of all boys. Shahaniki's large family had come to Istanbul from a small village, Sarai, in Yozgat province. The reason for the move was that they did not feel safe in their village. Her father had purchased a boom box, and the villagers of Sarai thought the boom box was a bomb. They called the police and he was arrested and jailed. I don't know for how long he was imprisoned, but upon his release they decided to move.

In 1971, a year after I had returned to America, Shahaniki and Hovannes were married in the Church of the Holy Mother on Istiklal Street in the Beyoglu district in Istanbul. In Armenian, the church is called Surp Astvasdatzin. Built in 1838, it was designed by the great Armenian architect Garabed Amira Balian. The interior, although dark with richly paneled wood, has a ceiling painted blue above the altar that resembles the night sky with stars. It is absolutely beautiful. Shahaniki and Hovannes eventually came to America, where he continued working as a designer of high-end jewelry and she began working as a seamstress, a trade she learned in secondary school in Yozgat.

Egsapet's son Sarkis and his wife, Sona, were also at the airport, as were their three sons. Sarkis was short and of medium build, with brown hair and dark, expressive eyes. Sona was taller than he, and though overweight and missing a few front teeth, had been without doubt a beauty in her youth with her translucent olive skin and beautiful hazel eyes. Their sons were Arto, the eldest, probably sixteen years old, Ashod, about ten, and Sevan, seven or eight years old. The eldest was learning how to be an auto mechanic, like his father, and the younger two were still in school, students at one of the best schools in the city. Sona came from a well-known family, the Findiklians, and spoke fluent French. Her brother, Aram Findiklian, was a renowned brain surgeon, with a medical office on Pangalti Street.

I stayed in Egsapet's home the entire time I was in Istanbul. We did a lot of sightseeing while I was there. One memorable day trip was to Kanala Ada, which at that time had a large Armenian population. It was a beautiful island with an Armenian church and a school. On another occasion, Egsapet took me to the French Hospital where she had worked for many years in the maternity ward, emptying bedpans and doing other menial chores. A young nun hurriedly opened the door, looked out at us, and nervously eyed the Turkish workmen who were on a scaffold repairing the exterior of the building. They looked at her and then whispered something in Turkish and laughed. She hurriedly shut the door.

Egsapet, having lived most of her adult life in Istanbul, had never been to Topkapi or the Dolmabahce Palace. One fine day we decided to go. Suddenly, in one of the private rooms of Sultan Abdul Hamid II, with no guards around, Egsapet decided to sit on the gilded commode of the infamous murderer of 250,000 Armenians. Squatting and lifting up the skirt of her dress, she sighed with an enormous smile on her face and said in Turkish, "It's a shame that I already relieved myself this morning." We kept pleading with her to get up, but she took her time, basking in this moment of glory.

On another day, we visited the Armenian cemetery to pay our respects to members of her family interred there. An Armenian gravedigger, middle aged, sinewy, of medium height, with a heavily lined face, and wearing a small, brown workman's cap, pulled me over to one side. Egsapet, who was now someplace else, had told him that I was visiting from America. He spoke to me firmly in Armenian: "Go back to America. This is a terrible country!" I told him I understood what he said. Looking back, I think now that perhaps he feared I was going to marry somebody there and stay.

I thought back to a day in September of 1955, fifteen years earlier, when I was in Ms. Donaldson's English class at Mission High School. It was a free reading day. I had picked up a copy of *Time* magazine and while thumbing through it came upon a small photograph of a group of very angry, young Turkish men, fists raised and screaming. Reading the accompanying article, I learned of a riot in Istanbul. In the course of the riot, the Armenian cemetery had been targeted and corpses defiled as the mob searched for buried treasure. To say I was outraged is an understatement. I wondered if this gravedigger, who told me to go back to America, was working in the cemetery when the riot happened.

Years later, I learned the backstory of the photograph. The riot took place on September 6 and 7, 1955, when the entire Greek community of Istanbul would be destroyed. The government under the leadership of the prime minister at the time, Adnan Menderes, had instigated the riot. Encouraging bands of Turkish youth to go through Greek, Armenian, and Jewish neighborhoods to demolish businesses, the government armed these thugs with acetylene torches, clubs, spades, pick axes, dynamite, and gasoline. To put the fear of God into the residents in these neighborhoods, these criminals went through the streets howling and carrying the Turkish red flag with the white star and sickle moon. They broke plate glass windows and did all kinds of other horrendous damage. Screams of their victims pierced the night along with the sounds of ambulances and police cars. In eight hours of September 6 and 7, 1955, hundreds of millions of dollars worth of property was destroyed and countless businessmen were wiped out. I wonder how many people heard of this tragedy. I think not very many. The article in *Time* magazine was so minute, it's a wonder I spotted it.

This unbelievable destruction started in Salonika, birthplace of the founder of the Turkish Republic, Kemal Ataturk. A rumor had spread that a bomb had been hurled at the former home of Kemal Ataturk by Greek terrorists. The fact is that only one window had been broken, by a bomb thrown at the Turkish consulate in Salonika. Later, it was discovered that the Greeks were not responsible, but the action had been planned and carried out by the Turkish government headed by Adnan Menderes, the prime minister. He was executed in 1960, not for his nefarious activities in destroying the Greek community of Istanbul but rather in the aftermath of a coup.

To make this event even more personal, my friend Armenuhi Hovanesian, who is an instructor at City College of San Francisco, told me of the experiences of her mother, Siran Hovanesian, who had been in Istanbul at the time of the riots. Siran, a beautiful young woman had been living with relatives. Everybody in the apartment heard the screaming on the street. Crowds of men were taunting and calling for Greek and Armenian girls to come out of their apartments or they would come inside and get them. The relatives hurriedly ushered Siran into one of the bedrooms and told her to get under the bed and stay there, perfectly still, until the whole thing subsided. Siran was terrified as first the front door was bashed in, and then she heard thundering footsteps on the stairs as the men stormed the building. More doors were broken and then screams came from adjacent apartments all night long. The next morning Siran and her relatives found out that girls in the apartment building and all over the neighborhood had been raped, many with bottles shoved into their vaginas. Hospitals all over the city were treating the victims.

Those sad days seemed to be over as everything about my visit with Egsapet and her family was so much fun. She wanted me to experience her everyday life. One day was set aside to go to a *hamam* or Turkish bath. It wasn't too far away from the apartment, so off we went. The Turkish woman who collected Egsapet's money was dressed in full black pants and wore a headscarf tied with a knot. We took off our clothes and went into the large, circular room with the domed skylight overhead. Egsapet proceeded to wash my hair and then I washed hers and scrubbed her back. I couldn't help but notice two beautiful young Turkish women: tall and slim with long, light brown hair. They were using some kind of a salve to remove their pubic hair and all the while were talking in whispers and washing their slim bodies, basking in the hot vapors and perfume.

They reminded me of the beautiful young girls described in the lines of the poem *Oriental Bath* by Daniel Varoujan. He had been one of the victims on April 24, 1915, the beginning of the genocide of the Armenian people throughout the Ottoman Empire. His poem perfectly describes what I experienced that day.

Inside the bath their low melodious voices

And their soft breath turn to muffled bells.

And as the vapor rises within

The bath, like moistened veils clinging

Along their naked bodies, which now start to pearl

With sweat, their eyes glow with a fine warm luster,

Like brilliant stars seen through a foggy sky.

Houris at their baths!...[1]

I grew very fond of Egsapet during my time in Istanbul. She had such an easy rapport with everybody: with the Kurdish woman, dressed all in black, who sold yogurt on the street; with the Turkish cab driver who told her of his cancer and his philosophical take on his chances to beat it; with the elegant silver-haired gentleman from her village who paid us a visit one afternoon, bringing her a bag of fresh apricots.

The relaxed atmosphere in Egsapet's apartment changed dramatically when her cousin Armenouhi Atamian, who also happened to be my father's first cousin, visited from Nice. Both her husband and her brother had recently died. She brought two large suitcases filled with her deceased husband's clothing to give away, and wrapped in tissue was a beautiful purple sweater that she had knitted and presented to me. I was thrilled to get it.

The first thing she did was look at the bedroom in disgust, more I think to show me that she didn't approve of such shoddy housekeeping. It hadn't bothered me at all until she pointed out how dusty the room was. Why, she asked, had Egsapet kept a bowl of fresh fruit on the table near an open window that attracted hoards of mosquitoes? I could see that Egsapet was humiliated by this fault-finding by her cousin and told her so.

Later I found out the source of Armenouhi's brittleness. She had not spoken with her brother Merger for some time over a stupid disagreement, and then he died. They had shared so much history together through the horrible times of the deportations and the return to their village from the exile.

My brother Arthur had visited Armenouhi and her husband in Nice and told me that her husband had been verbally abusive to her. He was definitely not the kind and loving man her brother was. Armenouhi was more distraught about her brother's death then her husband's demise. The torture she was putting herself through was a lesson to me about doing one's best to reconcile with family members before it's too late.

Egsapet was able to get over her hurt feelings. Armenouhi was her friend once more and even invited her cousin to give up her apartment in Istanbul and move to Nice. Egsapet felt she was too old for such a big move and she did not want to leave her family. Both of them had suffered greatly during the genocide. Armenouhi and her equally beautiful sister Vartouhi weren't deported with the other villagers. Instead, the sisters were kidnapped by Chechen irregulars and separated from their families. These men had been hired by the Turkish government to kill all of the able-bodied Armenian men and boys. Both girls were rescued in 1918 from their sexual enslavement. Egsapet's history was as eventful. She was forcibly abducted by a Turk during the deportations and raped. Subsequently, she gave birth to a blue-eyed son who was taken from her immediately afterward. He was known in her family as the "lost boy."

Egsapet rescued herself when a member of the philanthropic organization the Armenian General Benevolent Union came to the house where she was being held hostage. She burst out of the back room when she heard someone say that he was looking for Armenian children. She shouted at the top of her voice, "Here I am!" Egsapet was placed in an orphanage and while there met another orphan, Haroutiun Baharyan, who would later become her husband.

They came to Istanbul, where he apprenticed in the construction trades and became such a good designer that his plans were used all over the city for public works. And then he was gone. Egsapet told me, "One night, we were sleeping side by side, and when I woke up in the morning he was dead." He was just forty years old. Now, she had four sons to rear on her own. One of her boys had already died from crib death. Another son, named Grigor, was drafted into the Turkish army. While in service, he fell from a horse and his injuries were such that he had to be hospitalized. There he contracted pneumonia, which proved to be fatal.

When I was a youngster, Egsapet had written to my parents and asked them to send her penicillin for Grigor, as she couldn't afford it. My parents were extremely distressed that they were not able to do so. When penicillin was made available at the hospital there was only a limited amount. It would either go to him or to the young man who was also very ill next to him. Grigor requested that it be given to the young man because he was married and a father of three children while Grigor was single. That was the reason for the gift of life.

Egsapet raised her sons on her own for many years, working in the maternity ward of the French hospital. It was only when the boys were old enough and had jobs that she finally stopped working. We learned of Egsapet's death in 1974. Years later I heard from Shahaniki of the deaths of Sona and Sarkis. They were both buried in Istanbul. Their sons now live in Vienna. Arto repairs cars as his father, Sarkis, did in Turkey. Ashod works as a translator, and Sevan works at the airport.

✠ ✠ ✠ ✠

JUNE 3, 2009. My reverie was broken when I looked at my watch and wondered when Armen and the cab would arrive, as the ferryboat would be departing soon. Suddenly Armen rushed into the lobby of the hotel and we got into the cab and took off. The driver of the cab took many chances, honked his horn repeatedly, and maneuvered in and out of tight spots. I was in a heightened state of anxiety. Outwardly, I was keeping it together, but inside I was wondering if once again, as in 1970, I would not be able to see my father's village. We arrived at the terminal and there was Armen's friend and our driver, Mazhar Unsal, and Mazhar's wife, Ayfer. Their car went up the ramp and we entered the passenger section of the ferryboat. Mazhar, in his early sixties, was a very tall, soft-spoken man. He studied at Virginia Tech, earning a PhD in mechanical engineering. He was very accommodating and helpful. Eyfer was short and chubby, with a full head of brown hair, and had a dynamic, bubbly personality. She was an expert cook and very knowledgeable about the cuisine of Turkey.

Ayfer calmed down, as she was also upset wondering if we would arrive on time, and offered us a snack of fruit she had prepared. A group of Arabs were sitting near us in the passenger section lustily enjoying a lunch of *lahmajoon* (a form of Middle Eastern pizza), and Ayfer made fun of them under her breath. All I saw was a group of men obviously enjoying one another's company and good food.

When the boat docked, we got into Mazhar's car and began the drive on the highway that would take us to the village. It was a very hot day. Then we arrived, and I was so happy to see the sign marking the entrance of the village was still Keramet, which means "God's blessing." This was an apt name for the village, as the Armenians all felt blessed living there. Armen took a picture of me pointing to the sign. Then we began to drive up the high hill of Keramet until we finally stopped and got out.

Very few of the homes that we saw were the original structures built by the Armenians. Bulgarian Turkish refugees and other Turks who had come from the Balkans in 1989 built the relatively newer buildings. The conditions in Bulgaria made it impossible for them to remain as a result of the campaign of assimilation instigated by the Bulgarian government in 1984 under the leadership of Zhivhov.

In 1986, a former Kerametsi, Hadji Antrias Manoogian, visited the village with his two daughters and son-in-law. They had left France from Marseilles by plane, and when they reached Turkey, they rented a car that the son-in-law drove. Upon reaching the village, Antrias passed himself off as a Frenchman who could speak Turkish. The Turks were living in the burnt-out ruins of the Armenian homes—ruins that went back to the period of the massacres and deportations. When Antrias asked for information about the former inhabitants of the village, the Turks replied that it had been an Armenian village, but the Armenians left after burning their homes in 1915. Antrias and his family did not comment on this distorted account of the Armenian deportations. Antrias also noted that none of the streets were intact as they had been before 1915.

As Armen and I walked around, I saw that the *hamam* was still intact. My father told me that the villagers had put in the foundation before the massacres and deportations and that the Turks completed it after the Armenians were gone. I also noticed the lovely pink paving stones near the village center.

In 1939, François Balsan, a French wool merchant (1902–1972), traveled through historic Armenia. This area is about a thousand miles east of the southern Marmara region where Keramet is located, but what he discovered on his trip is relevant to what I discovered in Keramet. Balsan was a great admirer of the Turkish regime prior to World War II and not sympathetic to the Armenians at all. Setting aside his own prejudices, he objectively documented eyewitness accounts of the local people about the massacres and deportations in the book he wrote about his travels (*Les Surprises du Kurdistan, Coll. Voyages et Aventures*, Paris, J. Susse, 1944). He described the ruins of Armenian towns, villages, and monasteries and quoted specifically the words of Turkish officials who had declared, "It is necessary to destroy all traces of Armenians from Turkish soil." From what I saw in Keramet, they had done a thorough job.

Armen and I walked over to the village center and he asked the people enjoying their tea whether there was an Armenian church still standing. They said no, there was no church, but they directed us to where it once was, the center of the village. Now there stood a nondescript building containing a health clinic and wedding reception hall. We noticed a staircase on one side going up to the second floor. Saint Minas was a tall, solidly built church. It had a second floor and a balcony that the women of the village could access by going up the side stone steps to the little door that they opened.

We walked back to the village square where one of the most dramatic natural sites was the huge tree where my grandfather, the village butcher, would display the meat for sale. We asked the Turks congregated in the café about the old Turkish school. They pointed up the hill and said there was a house (my grandfather's) that had been torn down many years before to build the Turkish school. But the school had also been torn down.

What a water-rich village! You could turn on a faucet at a public fountain and ice cold water gushed out. Looking down from our high vantage point, we could see the huge freshwater lake of Iznik. Surrounding it were orchards of very old olive trees. In the alleyways adjacent to where we walked were dirt pathways and pointed slabs of building material that protruded from the ground. I thought that perhaps they could have been from the foundations of the long gone Armenian-made buildings.

We left Keramet and drove to the town of Iznik (formerly Nicaea). We would not stay but drove through it, noticing as we did the huge wall from the Byzantine era that is one of the distinguishing characteristics of the city. We would return later that afternoon, but now we set our course for Mekece and the train station about twenty miles away. The setting was absolutely spectacular. What must my dad and his family have been thinking in 1915 as they traversed these roads by oxen-driven cart to get to Mekece, from which they would be deported to the Syrian desert? Surely they thought, as I did, what an absolutely beautiful country they lived in. We drove past the towns of Kaynarca, Bilecik, Beseviler, and Cerkesli, and then we reached the train station standing next to the new, dark gray asphalt of a modern highway. Huge trucks kept whizzing by, so I could barely position myself across the road to take photographs, but I did.

Armen commented that the station, a beautifully painted yellow building, was stylistically similar to German-built stations elsewhere in Turkey, most of them constructed before and during the First World War. The train station was empty, not like it was in 1915, when under chaotic conditions hundreds and hundreds of Armenians arrived, many in a total state of panic. They were pushed into the cattle cars that would take them on their last journeys, caravans to oblivion. That was the plan!

Afterward, we drove back to Iznik and stopped at the tiny mall where one shop after another sold Kutahya-style pottery, jewelry, and collectibles. I bought some souvenirs to take home with me. Then we had a bite to eat, after which Armen and I went over to the ruins of the Greek Church of Saint Sophia, now a "museum," which was totally gutted. I was curious to know what tourists were supposed to look at as I studied the ravaged interior.

Nicaea was once the home of the beautiful and priceless Church of the Dormition dating back to the ninth century and decorated with very fine mosaics. It was probably the most important Byzantine cathedral in Asia Minor. During the Turkish War of Independence (1922–1923) and under the leadership of Cemal Mustapha, Turks laid waste to Christian communities in this area, and the church was burnt to the ground and destroyed in 1922. What an incalculable loss!

After our short visit to Iznik, we went back toward Keramet, driving by the towns of Karasu, Kuredere, and Boyalika. I saw a gushing waterfall, about my height, coming out of the rocks very near the village. I got out and took pictures and gathered some soil from the ground, which I placed into a little plastic bag that I would bury later at my father's gravesite in Colma, California.

Ayfer had reserved rooms for us at a hotel called Otel Villa Familia. That's where we stayed until morning, when the second day of our journey would begin. Everywhere we went Ayfer would select the dishes that best represented the area where we dined. We had a lovely dinner of appetizers at the Otel that evening. The next day, after a continental breakfast, we drove around Lake Iznik to Soloz and Yeni Soloz.

I had promised a friend, Stephan Karadian, that I would go to this area, as his father, Sahag, had been born in Yeni Soloz. We drove high up the mountain to get to the site. How beautiful was the setting: lush green orchards of olive trees and puffy mists of clouds lingering on the tops of the mountains.

We parked near a school where luckily the children were at recess, as their regular teacher was absent and there was no substitute. While in the schoolyard girls thirteen to fifteen years old gathered around Ayfer and delightedly spoke to her about all kinds of things. The younger children, six or so in number, gathered around Armen, and soon he had them singing at the top of their lungs as he videotaped them.

Frere Jacques, Are You Sleeping?
Are you sleeping,
Are you sleeping?
Brother John?
Brother John?
Morning bells are ringing,
Morning bells are ringing,
Ding, ding, dong,
Ding, ding, dong.

After the sing-along, Armen started asking them about their beautiful village and about the Armenians who had once lived here. They all concurred that it had once been an Armenian village. When he inquired further and asked them what had happened to the Armenians, they replied that one day, they had left the village and were never seen again.

Interestingly enough, there were two large gravestones tossed haphazardly near where the children had congregated around Armen. They all walked over to the gravestones that had once been in a cemetery. One was sticking out of the ground and the other was lying flat with the Armenian writing exposed. One of the girls told Armen that the square-topped gravestone was for a deceased male and the round-topped one was for a female.

Just before we left these very bright and inquisitive children, one of the older girls complained about the ugly newer buildings going up and how the demolished older buildings were much more beautiful. Maybe one day she'll become an architect.

Next, it was off to lunch in Gemlik. After driving for a while, we parked and walked over to the fish restaurant Boksor which, thanks to Ayfer's research, was the place to eat in Gemlik. As we sat next to the window of the restaurant, I marveled at the sea and thought about what a culturally diverse hub Gemlik had been before 1915. Twenty thousand Armenians lived in this port city, at that time. I wondered to myself if any Armenians lived there now.

Before we left Gemlik and drove to the ferry that would take us back to Istanbul, Armen told me that he wanted to videotape me reading, in Armenian translation, the Gaelic prayer that I had brought with me to Turkey. This I would read in respect to our million and a half martyrs who had been killed in the streets of their cities and villages, in the bedrooms of their homes, in their gardens, and on lonely roads. Their bodies dumped unceremoniously in gullies, in ditches, in wells, and in lakes, rivers, and seas. The prayer was for their souls, because when they were killed, there was no ceremony of any kind. Here is the prayer:

Gaelic Prayer

Deep peace of the running waves to you.

Deep peace of the flowing air to you.

Deep peace of the smiling stars to you.

Deep peace of the quiet earth to you.

Deep peace of the watching shepherds to you.

Deep peace of the Son of Peace to you.[2]

Keramet, Turkey, June 2009.
Sign at the entrance of the village.

Istanbul, summer 1970. Fishing in the Bosphorus. The Baharyans: Left to right: Ashod, Egsapet, Sarkis, and Sevan.

Silivri, Turkey, summer 1970. Left to right: Armenouhi Atamian, Ellen, Egsapet, Sevan, Sona, Sarkis, and Ashod.

Istanbul, summer 1970. Ellen and Egsapet in front of Saint Hiresoagabet Armenian Church (Saint Archangel Church).

Keramet Village, June 2009. Turkish bath. Armenians laid the foundation before deportation in 1915.

Keramet Village, June 2009. Villager and Ellen.

Mekece, Turkey, June 2009. Train station from which Armenians were taken by cattle cars in 1915 to Adana, Turkey, and then made to walk through Syria to their deaths.

Keramet Village, June 2009. Branch from which meat was hung for sale by Grandfather Markar, the village butcher.

Yeni Soloz, June 2009. School yard. No teacher and no substitute. Students gather around Ayfer Unsal. Ellen is wearing a baseball cap.

Yeni Soloz, June 2009. Tombstone near school yard. Name on tombstone: Mrs. Anna Danigian. "Men can toil as much as they can but it is in vain because God decides one's life . . ."

Bulgaria, August 1957. Garabed Haji Nigogos Papazian (center front row with family). Garabed compiled the statistics of Keramet. Far left, front row: Paris Mergerditch Karafilian visiting from Armenia.

Asnieres, France, 1992. On left: Shakeh Jasmine Samouelian. Her sister Anahid Nigogossian on right. They are the daughters of Hagop Nigogossian.

New York, 1940. On left: Florence Pashayan at 18 years of age. Her sister Rose Stewart on right. They are the daughters of Aghavni.

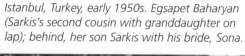

*France, May 9, 1953. Left to right:
Turvanda (Merger's wife), Kohar Markarian
(Sarkis's niece), Shakeh (daughter of Turvanda
and Merger), Alice Markarian (younger sister of
Kohar), and Merger Arekelian (Sarkis's first cousin).*

*Istanbul, Turkey, early 1950s. Grigor, Egsapet's
son, in dark robe in the hospital yard.*

*Istanbul, Turkey, early 1950s. Egsapet Baharyan
(Sarkis's second cousin with granddaughter on
lap); behind, her son Sarkis with his bride, Sona.*

Geary Street, San Francisco, 1975. Nazareth Bidanian (teacher and intellectual) in his office.

Bulgaria, 1986. Yezekel Ashirian, Sarkis's boyhood friend from Keramet Village.

Anjar, Lebanon, 1946. Sosse Shrikian, age 22, and fiancé, Nazareth Bidanian, age 29. Nishanduk (engagement photograph).

New York, 1988. Left to right: Vramshabouh Pashayan (born in Cengiler, Turkey), his wife, Florence Pashayan (daughter of Aghavni), and her sister-in-law Varsenig Topouzian (also born in Cengiler, Turkey).

San Francisco, April 1966. Marie Sanson, born in Corfu, Greece in 1922, the year of the "Great Catastrophe." Some of her relatives were from the Southern Marmara region.

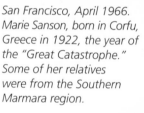

Paris, France, 1965. Left: Philip Taleur (Sarkis's cousin) and Arthur Minas (son of Sarkis).

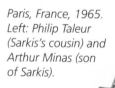

Karabash, an Anatolian sheepdog. Sarkis's family owned several.

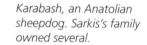

Pre-1915, there were well over one hundred Armenian villages in the province of Bursa. Above are the cities, towns, and villages that played an important role in the story of the Kerametsis.

CHAPTER 2

KERAMET
WHEN IT WAS AN
ARMENIAN VILLAGE

Picture taken in Keramet in 2009 showing a primitive oven similar to ones used by Keremetsis pre-1915.

I ENJOYED MY TRIP TO KERAMET IN 2009. However, there was little that gave me the sense of what it must have been like before 1915. For that, I have relied on the recollections of former Kerametsis, the most important of whom was my father, Deli Sarkis. First some physical description is necessary. Keramet lies in a fertile basin close to the eastern end of Lake Ascania or Ascanius (now Lake Iznik). This sweet-water lake is twenty miles in length. Keramet is bounded by ranges of hills and is west of the famous ancient city Nicaea, now called Iznik. Before 1915, Keramet boasted around 1,500 residents, mostly Armenian, with five Turkish families who spoke fluent Armenian. Because of its close proximity to Iznik, it was subjected to the same vicissitudes during times of political turbulence and upheaval. Keramet, like Iznik, is located on an extensive plain and at a juncture of roads leading through Asia Minor to Istanbul.

The entire region is incredibly water rich. There were at one time thirty-eight hot springs near Keramet that emptied into Lake Iznik. The town of Yalova, near Keramet, had many hot springs, and so did the town of Kaplaga. I saw one hot spring near the entrance to the village of Keramet in 2009. Men and children were swimming in its waters while women sat at picnic tables and a vendor, in a small kiosk, sold food.

Before 1915, there were a number of Armenian villages near the lake: Cengiler, Ortakev, Yenikoy, Norkek, and Keramet on one side of the lake, and on the opposite side Bayni, Karsak, Gurla, and Soloz. Some distance away was the large city of Adabazar that had an Armenian population of twenty thousand, while the smaller towns of Orhangazi and Gemlik had large communities also. There were well over one hundred Armenian villages in the province of Bursa.

Geographically, one stunning sight was the mountain near Bursa known in pre-1915 times as Keshishdagh or preacher mountain, from the Turkish words *keshish* (preacher) and *dagh* (mountain). It is now called Uludag.

Many of the Armenian villagers engaged in farming. So much was grown. Besides olives, cultivated in and around the village of Keramet, they grew grapes, wheat, barley, oats, millet, bitter vetch, maize, sesame, flax, hemp, cotton, tobacco, kidney beans, broad beans, chickpeas, lentils, melon, watermelon, and chestnuts. Rose oil was extracted from the flower.

There was a winery and an olive oil processing facility. Many of the men worked as farmhands, mule drivers, oxen drivers, and wheat threshers. Just about all of the villages in the region were involved in sericulture. Mulberry trees were abundant, which made this an ideal center for raw silk production. This was a labor-intensive process, beginning with the production of the eggs, through to hatching the worms and the cocoon stage. These processes involved considerable risks. All residents of Keramet raised silkworms. Aghavni Manoogian said that they raised silkworms (called *bocegi*) in the attic of one of their three homes in Keramet. Women did most of this work to supplement the family income. When the larvae hatched, the women in each family would gather the mulberry branches and assume responsibility for raising the silkworms.

Between 1888 and 1905, a total of 73.3 percent of the Bursa-region silk producers were either Greek or Armenian. The Armenians controlled the silkworm egg and cocoon phases of the industry. [3]

This was a multiethnic region, with Greek, Turkish, and Armenian villages coexisting. The head of a Muslim village was known as *Muhtar* and the man in charge of a Christian village was known as *Kiaya*. The Greek villages of Guzderbend and Derbend were a few hours walking distance from Keramet, and my grandfather invited musician friends from these villages to play at the weddings.

This is what my father, Deli Sarkis, who was ten years old in 1915, remembered of his village.

"Our history was passed down orally. I was told that we Armenians were brought here many centuries ago, from Armenia, to work the land. Our church, Saint Minas, was rebuilt in 1835 into a very substantial and beautiful structure. Our clan, the Mesrobian, was the largest in the village, comprising 150 persons. My father, Markar, came from a family of seven brothers and one sister. Besides my father, there were Garabed, Arakel, Alexan, Ovannes (the eldest), Megerditch Agha (otherwise known as Badveli, as he was an ordained minister), and Zahatel (who was also known as Shapatabah, because he was a Seventh-day Adventist). Zahatel owned the flour mill that was near a stream. Their sister was Osanna. Arakel was the father of my cousins Armenouhi, Vartouhi, and Merger.

Garabed was the father of my cousins Zareh, Stepan, Krikor, and Faron. My eldest uncle, Ovannes, died before the massacres and deportations of 1915, as he was a sick man. Most of my other uncles, my aunt, and my father were either killed outright by the Turks or died during the deportations to the Syrian deserts.

My father, Markar, forty years old in 1915, was of medium height, sturdily built, and had a luxurious brown mustache. He was a renowned hunter and the lone butcher of Keramet. He also set bones, both animal and human, and treated sick animals with herbs. He cared for animals in Turkish villages, too. At weddings, he'd play the bagpipes (in Armenian the instrument is called *parkapzouk*). His hunting skills, however, brought him the most fame. One day he killed an animal with an exquisite hide. He cured the skin and then took it to Constantinople. He looked up his friend Davit, and with his connections he sold the animal skin for forty gold pounds, which was an enormous amount of money in those days.

Another noted episode occurred when my father had killed a number of foxes. After curing the hides he displayed them on a wall in the barn. This was so people could select the hides they would purchase. There were twenty hides, or so my father thought. But when he counted them, he saw that mysteriously there were twenty-one. He studied the hides closely and saw that a fox was up there with the other hides playing dead. Clever animal! We kept our hens and chickens in the barn, too.

My father never owned a horse. He felt it was bad luck to own one. We did have a donkey. My father made an *ambar* (storage bin) that was six by twelve feet in size. This was where we kept our grain.

After I had returned to the village, in 1919, following the deportations, I sold the *ambar* to a Turk from a neighboring village for five gold pounds. It was then that I found my father's old musket that he had hidden in the gutter on the roof.

My mother's birth name was Elizabeth Kupjian. She was of medium height and well proportioned. In 1915, she was probably thirty-four years old. Mother had three sisters and one brother, Alexan. He was six feet tall and very handsome. When the war broke out he was drafted into the

Turkish army. He was not married at the time, and never returned. Mother was extremely well liked by everyone in the village, and was called *Hatun Abla* (sister, Hatun).

As mentioned before, I was ten years old in 1915. My brother Haroutiun (also called Artin) was twelve. My brother Nazar was sixteen, blond, blue-eyed, tall, and slim. My eldest brother, Minas, was eighteen. Baby Bedros died in the village of a fever before the deportations. He was buried in the graveyard outside the village. When I came back in 1919, I visited his gravesite. Of all my siblings, only Haroutiun and I survived the deportations. Nazar made it through the Syrian wilderness but died in Tell Keif, Iraq.

All of the boys in our family looked up to our eldest brother, Minas. He helped my father in the butcher shop and also helped in planting crops. He took care of us. When he got his hair cut, he would take us with him and the barber cut our hair for free.

What a terrific dancer he was! My mother and Minas would dance at all the village weddings. Greek and Turkish villagers invited him to dance at their weddings, too. One was in the Turkish village of Chakurlu (now known as Cakur).

I remember the last day I saw Minas. He was leaving for the city of Bursa, as he had been drafted into the Turkish army. My mother packed him a big lunch, wrapping it up in a cloth sack. I knew she was going to miss him very much, as he was her favorite. We boys followed after him for a considerable time as he walked away from the village. When he and a couple of other boys, who had also been drafted, came up to the top of a hill, they threw rocks at us in farewell.

Minas was engaged to Ariknazan. In Syria, during the time of the deportations, she disappeared. Before that happened, however, and while he was still in the Turkish army, Minas had heard about the deportations and he deserted. He was near Keramet when he was killed. A Turkish farmer shot him dead when he caught him stealing some fruit.

I was too young to understand what the men of the village talked about politically. I do know that my father belonged to the Tashnak Party and my eldest brother, Minas, was a Hunchak. I have no doubt that we learned of the massacres against the Armenians in the eastern provinces perpetrated by Sultan Abdul Hamid II in 1894–1896, and the other terrible massacre perpetrated by the Young Turks in 1909. Why else would the men of our village join political parties? We had no other choice.

All of the girls of our extended family and the village girls went through torturous times during the deportations. Egsapet Baharyan, the granddaughter of Ovannes, my father's eldest brother, survived. Another survivor was my cousin Faron, who was about to be married before the deportations. But sadly her fiancé became sick and died. During the deportations, she walked all the way to the Sinjar in Mesopotamia and was taken in and remained with the Yazidis for three years. Her brother Zareh rescued her from the Yazidis in 1918. She was married off to an older Armenian man who was over fifty, while she was only sixteen years of age. She ended up in Bulgaria, where she died many years later. Her Armenian neighbors remembered her as being a sweet and happy woman.

Yezekel Tenekeji Ashirian was my best friend in my boyhood. Yezekel's father worked with tin and made pipes for kitchen stoves. His eldest sister, Arusak, married an Arab during the deportation period. She divorced him after the war and married Zareh, my first cousin. Siranoush, Yezekel's sister, disappeared during the deportations. Another of my close playmates was Emine Ali Chavoush, a Turkish girl who lived with her family in Keramet. I don't know what happened to her or her family, because when I came back to the village in 1919 they were no longer there.

Our family home was made of wood and was two stories high. It was located on the high hill of the village, close to the pasture where our two hundred sheep were taken for grazing. My brother Nazar, who always carried a gun, and his helper, a Turkish boy, took the sheep to pasture accompanied by our four dogs: Karabash, Yalabash, Akbash, and Sarabash. Our dogs were very protective of the sheep and would ward off predators. We would take food to Nazar when he was in the hills.

As soon as spring came, the sheep were sheared. Everybody in the village did this at the same time. The sheep in Keramet were not very heavy and did not have big tails. My father cured the skin to make leather. We had a shoemaker in the village. Women would spin the wool. We didn't waste any part of the sheep. Our father would give each of us a baby lamb when we were youngsters. They were our pets, but they still would have to go to the pasture with the other sheep. When it snowed in the winter, our sheep were kept near the house.

We owned an acre of land near the house. In the spring, seasonal workers would come to our homestead and to others in the village to turn and fertilize the soil. My mother would feed these workers when they worked on our land.

Our home, so far up the hill of Keramet, had a magnificent view of Lake Iznik. We had glass panes in the windows and a knocker on the front door. When you entered, there was a short hallway leading into the living room. Built-in divans circled this room. Cushioned backrests made for comfortable seating. The fireplace was set into the wall. We ate in this room. Our dining table was big, round, and about fifteen inches off the floor. We ate with wooden spoons and put our food in wooden bowls. Our spoons were made of different kinds of wood because of the wear and tear on them.

Our bedrooms were upstairs. The floors were covered, but not with woven carpets, as we did not weave carpets in Keramet. Each of us had his own quilted *doshag* (woolen mattress). We would lay our mattresses on the floor when it was time to sleep, covering ourselves with our *vermags* (comforters). In the morning, the mattresses and comforters were put away. Once a week, sheets were changed.

We lived simply. There were no books in our house. We didn't own a clock but kept time by the direction of the sun. Kerosene lamps provided us with light at night.

If I wasn't out playing or fishing with my two friends, Yezekel and Emine, I was watching my mother prepare food. I loved to watch her, and maybe that's why I have enjoyed cooking my entire life. Here are the names of the fish that lived in our fresh water lake: Sarabaluk, Yayunbaluk, Teekenje, Eleekjuk, Airdekzuk, and Akbaluk.

Since we didn't own an oven, mother would take her prepared dough in a bread pan to one of the ten ovens in the village. We called our bread *somun*. Mother would put sesame seeds in the dough that gave the bread a wonderful flavor. After baking, the bread rose very high and was brown and delicious. Mother always gave the baker a loaf of bread as payment.

My mother was very hardworking, and so were the other women in the village. Even when she was pregnant with my youngest brother, Bedros, she continued working hard. She always had helpers, though. They were girls from the village. I remember the name of one of them—Sophia. She would be with my mother every day. Mother prepared food in the *muslak* (kitchen) and washed our bowls and spoons there. When she wasn't preparing our meals, she would make butter, cheese, and yogurt.

Mother would spin the wool from our sheep, take care of the silkworms, and make our clothes on a sewing machine. Food was preserved in our cellar where dried fruit, pickles, and cheese were kept. Tea was the beverage of choice. We drank coffee occasionally, and it came from Yemen. Since we grew tobacco in the village, the men rolled their own cigarettes. I started smoking while quite young, as I had colitis and my father thought the nicotine would help. It did!

Here are some of the foods we ate: breakfast consisted of *targhana* or yogurt soup, lunch was mostly stews, while dinner was our big meal. We ate *batlejan* (stuffed baked eggplant), *bameya* (okra stew with onions and tomato sauce), bulgar pilaf (coarse bulgar wheat, onion, with chicken broth), *bastarma* (dried spiced beef), *soudjookh* (a highly spiced sausage), *bastegh* (a paste prepared with fruit and sugar), *sarma* (grape leaves stuffed with ground lamb), dolma (green peppers stuffed with tomatoes, onions and ground lamb), and *barbunya* (a red mullet which is a kind of bean).

I remember a communal activity involving the women of the village. A dozen women would go to the grape orchard and stay there for a week. My father would put up tents for the women. There they would make *bastegh* (homemade fruit leather made from grape juice thickened with flour). They cooked it and spread the mixture in the sun to dry. They also made jam or paste from *kestene* (chestnuts), candied the chestnuts or roasted them.

The women of our village dressed very colorfully. Mother kept her long, brown hair tied back and loose. She always wore full, mostly black, pants. Her waist-length jackets were long-sleeved, buttoned down the front, and made of colorful cotton prints. While working outdoors, Mother kept her hair covered in cotton *yazmas*, which were made of a fabric like cheesecloth, dyed, and edged in delicate needle lace flowers. Cotton *shalvars* (pants) were worn in the house and fields. Silk was used for special occasions. At night, Mother wore a loose nightgown.

Women wore the family wealth in the form of gold jewelry. The men of our village wore red fezzes, as did the Turks. I wore loose, black *shalvar* (pants) with a full shirt tucked in. The pants were held up with a cord fitted into the loops of the waist.

The young girls of our village wore ankle-length dresses. Their long hair was braided. The girls of our village were kept incredibly busy working alongside their mothers doing household chores. All girls knew how to make needle lace that formed an important part in the ornamentation of items they made for their trousseaux.

Our village had a center with a café. Our barber had a small space in the café. The blacksmith shop was also located in the center. The blacksmith cleaned and repaired copper pots along with all of his other important activities.

My father was the only butcher in Keramet. His "shop" consisted of a flat, smooth tree trunk on which he would prepare carcasses of slaughtered animals, mostly lamb or goat, which he would then hang on hooks from the thick branch of a two-hundred-year-old tree. No meat was left on the branch at night. He would sell it all. Villagers could purchase meat from him on credit. We did have a general store. We had laid the foundation for the *hamam* (bathhouse) just before the massacres and deportations. It was up the hill from the center.

We had a school in which all grade levels were taught. The girls were separated from the boys, even though we shared the same building. All of our teachers were men. We read and wrote in Ottoman Turkish (with Arabic letters). We learned to read and write in Armenian, too, but were not taught Armenian history. We also learned arithmetic.

We had no doctors in the village; children came down with chicken pox and measles. We used herbs for treating all kinds of ailments. My father treated people who had bad burns with herbs.

Some families in our village were very poor. The other villagers would help these families by sending them food from their tables delivered by their children.

Since there was so much water in Keramet, bathing was no problem. We could bathe in the hot or cold springs near the lake. Our village women had a special day when only they would bathe. Our Turkish villagers bathed in the stream near our church. We had an outhouse near our home and we used rags to wipe ourselves.

Our traditions were very important to us. *Vartavar*[4] took place in August. In our village, we children called it *Churpoteek*. We would go from house to house and the women of the village would douse us with water. By the end of the day, we were soaked but happy. Another celebration was *Diarnentarach*.[5] All of the villagers would bring firewood to a central location. A large bonfire was started and we held hands circling the fire and singing songs. This took place on February 14, or the Day of the Presentation of Christ at the Temple.

The Festival of *Vidjak*[6] took place from the day of Ascension until the Saturday of Pentecost. The girls of Keramet always looked forward to this time. Boys were not privy to what occurred and they were not allowed in the ceremonies. I remember the joyfulness and an older woman telling the fortunes of the girls."

I interrupt my father's recollections here so the reader will understand more fully about what happened during the Festival of *Vidjak*. Here is a quotation from the book *Your Brother's Blood Cries Out* that beautifully describes this event:

> She was there when all the village girls went singing and carrying the large clay jug to fill with water from seven fountains. Ah, how the girls laughed and sang at every opportunity by the bubbling clear water! Then they came back, cautiously carrying the full jug, and each of them threw something inside: a brooch,

a ring, a glass pearl. And she, poor Araksi from below the river, had thrown in a simple button. All at once, with closed eyes, each girl had made a wish from the bottom of her heart, a wish that was dearest to each one. Then they had blocked the opening of the jug with flowers picked from seven different meadows and, finally, they had hidden it in the corner of a garden under the light of the stars. Stars of happiness had to shine on the wishes thrown into the jug to make them come true. Playing and singing, the girls had watched over their jug so that the village boys could not come and take it and demand multi-colored eggs in exchange for its return. They kept the jug until the day of Vidjak, the day before Pentecost. Then they had gathered, dressed in their best finery with ribbons in their braided hair, at Father Mesrob's, who was officiating at the holiday this year. Full of anticipation and joy they had danced around the jug, they had sung and made a doll with beautiful clothes, adorned her with jewelry and with coins, and they put her on the jug. She was Vidjak, the goddess of fortune, and in each heart beat the hope that she was going to hear Vidjak's voice.

Araksi thought of the doll with admiration as it was so beautiful. After that they had chosen a "queen" among the girls to carry the small goddess and to take the objects out of the jug. The queen they had chosen had naturally been Dirouhi, the daughter of Dr. Minassian. All the girls had filed passed the "queen." They had bowed and kissed the virgin Vidjak whom the "queen" had presented to them. Then the ritual of the oracle had begun. When each object was withdrawn from the jug by the queen, an old woman with covered eyes sang ancient verses, so ancient nobody knew how old they were. Yesterday it had been the priest's old mother who had sung, and the girls had clapped their hands and were delighted or saddened according to the verse which was recited when her object was withdrawn." [7]

My father's recollections about village life begin again: "At Christmas time, our own *Gaghant Baba* (Santa Claus) would go street by street and talk to all the children. He would ask us what we wanted for Christmas. It didn't matter what we requested, we all got red shoes as presents. Our gifts to *Gaghant Baba* consisted of chickens, eggs, and cheese.

At Easter, which was our really big holiday, we dyed eggs with the skins of colorful vegetables, and we all tried to crack somebody else's hardboiled egg with one of our own to see who was the champion egg cracker. Church service was very special with the mass and the beautiful voices of the choir filling the sanctuary and beyond. My brother Haroutiun sang in the choir, as he had a wonderful voice.

We always looked forward to the visits by traveling storytellers in the winter. These storytellers were older men who were put up in a room at someone's home. When it was time for stories to be told, we would gather round, sitting on benches in a hall lit with kerosene lamps. We ate pastries and listened to humorous stories or fairy tales. I don't ever remember sad stories being told. In Armenian, a storyteller is a *hekiat,* and the Turkish for storyteller is *masalji.* Once we were visited by a traveling troop of Turkish actors who put on a play for us. On another occasion, someone even brought a phonograph player to our village.

The little girls of our village played with dolls. All of the children played with a lamb bone. One of us would toss the bone and the person who called the side won. Hide-and-seek was a popular game.

There were special rules for engagement and marriage. Aghavni Manoogian remembered living in the house of her future mother-in-law when she was engaged to her son. This was even before she began menstruating. Only after she began menstruating could she marry. This did not apply to all the girls, because Ariknazan did not live in our home when she was engaged to my brother Minas.

After an engagement announcement, the boy and girl were not allowed to see one another. One day, Ariknazan saw my brother while she was doing her chores in the village, and she dropped whatever she was carrying and started to cry. He helped her pick up everything and comforted her. He also walked with her to her house but remained back so that people could not see him.

When a girl was married in Keramet, she was given a gift of a beautiful silk brocade coat trimmed and lined in fox fur. Greek and Turkish villages had the same tradition. The coats were of ankle length and had long sleeves.

After the wedding ceremony, the bride would sit on a horse so that all the villagers could see her. Her *gunkahayr* (godfather) took her through the village as she rode the horse. The marriage celebrations lasted one week. Music consisted of the *davul* (drum) and *zurna* (reed pipe) played by a half dozen young musicians from the Greek village of Guzderbend."

An example of Aintab drawn work, a pillow front in ivory linen with silk thread embroidery embellishment, edged with needle lace. From the collection of the author's family.

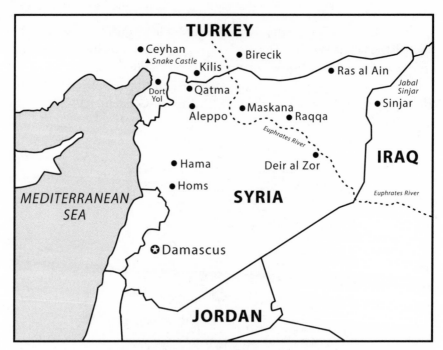

On May 27, 1915 the Young Turk government passed the Tehcir Law. Tehcir in Turkish means deportation. Its official name was Sevk Ve Iskan Kanunu (Dispatchment and Settlement Law). All Armenians not killed or kidnapped outright were driven by foot or cattle car to the deserts of Syria and Mesopotamia. Turks were deporting Armenians as early as March 2, 1915.

CHAPTER 3

MASSACRE
AND DEPORTATION

Arrest and kill Armenian males. Set the elderly, women, girls, and boys onto the roads with no protection, ending in either starvation, murder, or sexual degradation.

LATE SPRING 1915. Rumors had been spreading around the southern Marmara region for weeks before the deportation of the Armenians. While Turkish villagers did not spell it out for the fellow Greeks in the area, they did warn them of impending events: "Be careful. The atmosphere is very strange. Something is not right!"[8] Father Tomas Khengigian, the priest of Keramet, took these rumors very seriously, and what he and archdeacon Sarkis Gugherian did was only revealed a few years later under tragic circumstances. The treasures of the church of Saint Minas would be hidden.

SAINT MINAS REVEALS ITS SECRETS. When Father Tomas heard the rumors about the banishment of his people he had difficulty sleeping for days, worrying about his parishioners and his beloved church. He thought of a plan and spoke to archdeacon Sarkis Gugherian about the necessity of hiding the church's treasures. Sarkis Gugherian had been like a brother to him, sharing in the sacrament of holy orders and the liturgy, lovingly training the boy altar servers, visiting the sick, and helping Father Tomas with other parish duties.

Late one night, when the villagers were in their homes, the two men went to the church. Sarkis was carrying a kerosene lamp while Father Tomas unlocked the massive wooden door of the church and closed it as carefully as he could so as to not awaken the sleeping inhabitants of Keramet. When inside, they scanned the interior, looking at the dome that during services was illuminated by silver lamps and metaphorically represented the vault of heaven. Then they viewed the square layout of the church sanctuary that made the services visible from all points. Next they looked up at the windows that punctuated the high, wooden walls. They examined the *momavarutyan seghan* (candle-lighting table) along the right-side wall, filled with sand to prop up candles lit by parishioners before the church service.

Sarkis turned and looked up at the balcony reserved for the women, girls, and the choir and accessed only by stone steps on the outside of the building, and then they both stared straight ahead at the three altars which were horizontal slabs resting on a vertical column with steps to the right and left. The silk curtain, now drawn back, was used during Sunday services to separate the antechamber from the congregation. The left and right side aisles led into the vestry that in this church was behind the nave wall. The *avantadun* (vestry) was where the unleavened bread, vestments, and gold vessels were kept.

It took both of them a couple of trips back and forth to collect the crosses, some of them very heavy, and carry them into the vestry. When this was done, they prayed together, chanting. Father Tomas blessed each sacred object. Then, taking the cloth that was kept in the room, they individually wrapped the holy objects.

Shovels and tools were already there, and leaning up against one of the walls of the room was a very heavy, flat stone. Rolling up their sleeves, they began digging until a large hole was fashioned. Ever so gently, they placed the objects inside the hole with the container of the holy *meuron*[9] on top. They carried the stone and placed it over the hole, spending a lot of time smoothing over the area with dirt so that it looked undisturbed. Then they picked up the tools and Father Tomas closed the door of the vestry. Side by side, they walked up the central aisle of the church to the door, opened it, and went out into an incredibly beautiful, clear night. It was so lovely that for a moment they both put out of their minds what lay ahead.

BEGINNING OF THE END, 1915. Turkey had been at war for six months, having entered the war on Germany's side on October 29, 1914. My father's eldest brother, Minas, had already been conscripted into the army, as had his uncle Alexan.

This is what my father remembered of those terrible days. "One minute my friends and I were busy playing, jumping into Lake Iznik, and having fun, and then just like the snap of a finger, our lives changed. A messenger on horseback came galloping into our village from Constantinople and hurriedly posted a notice for all of us to read. The rumors proved to be true. It was signed by the minister of the interior, Talaat Pasha, notifying all of us to prepare for deportation for 'our own safety.' We were given two days to get our affairs in order. We would be going by train to areas away from the southern Marmara for the duration of the war. The train station was located at Mekece and was about thirty miles from the village.

All of the men of the village who were not working in the fields or in other areas gathered round the messenger as he nailed the notice onto the trunk of the tree high enough for all to read. Silence and then an unsettled murmuring, as if they couldn't quite comprehend what it was they had just read.

Somebody started yelling at the men nearby. 'Isn't it clear enough for you? You heard the rumors two weeks ago. They want to clean us out, kill us and take our property!' They stared at him in disbelief. 'I warned you,' he continued, 'that we needed to be prepared by stashing weapons! I knew this day would come. Now we have absolutely nothing with which to defend ourselves. We're going to be slaughtered like sheep. Well, don't just stand there, get your women and children ready!' He rushed off, disgusted.

The truth was there was no safe haven for us anywhere. The men went to their homes and told their families the news. The women en masse came pouring out of their homes from every direction to see the notice, and rushed over to the tree. Then, almost in unison, a great cry was heard from them that soon turned into a guttural wailing. In desperation, the women spoke to each other about how much time they had to get ready, as their first priority was the care of feeding of their families. What could they take, they screamed aloud, for such a journey? What bedding and food?

It wasn't just in Keremet, but similar occurrences were transpiring throughout the southern Marmara. Over all was a terrible specter like a cloud of poison. In the town of Bandirma near the Hellespont and close to the Sea of Marmara, a girl by the name of Elise Hagopian would write years later of the terrible experiences of her family in her memoirs *Rebirth*. They would also be transported by freight train away from their beloved Bandirma. What quicker way of disposing of people?

I think now that my father, Markar, realized he had to move as fast as possible, or else Turkish soldiers would be there soon and the killing would start: men would be separated from their families and killed in every way imaginable. Aghavni Manougian (born 1891) told me of the fate of the men of Keramet when we traveled back to the village a few years later. My mother and father worked as a team. There was no hysteria. They acted as if we were going on an outing. Mother supervised all of us as we gathered our bedding. We were sent to the cellar to get food that she would wrap up, in a bundle, to take with us. Luckily the sheep and the dogs were penned up next to our home and would be safe. But, there would be no one to look after the silkworms once we left the village.

Father hired someone who owned an ox-driven cart, and we piled on with our tent, bedding, and food. I looked back at our beloved Keramet as the cart rumbled down the hill of our village toward the main road leading to Iznik and then on to Mekece. After some time traveling, my father realized that he had forgotten some of his money. There were forty gold liras back at our house in addition to the hundred gold liras he had on his person. He told the driver to stop the movement of the cart, as he would have to walk back. This was the only money we had for our trip.

After a time, thankfully, he returned. The cart lumbered on and the landscape we saw was unbelievably beautiful, surrounded as we were by tall mountains and verdant valleys. Then we arrived in Mekece.

Absolute chaos greeted us. People were laden with quilts and bundles while children were screaming and running back and forth, looking for their parents. There were regular Turkish soldiers in khaki-colored uniforms that had large buttons, all wearing long boots and red fezzes on their heads and heavily armed. The soldiers began herding the men, women, and children, who had arrived on foot or on donkeys and carts, onto the cattle cars. Obediently, we did as we were told. There was no other option!

Thankfully, our family was able to stay together even though, like the others, we were roughly handled. There were Armenians from Adabazar, Armash, and Nicomedia (now Izmit), along with people from other towns and villages. Fear was palpable on the faces of all. We were all nervous and many were crying.

I had trouble breathing, as the boxcar was very hot and stank. We were crammed in so tight behind the slatted bars of the boxcar. No water to drink! Two piles of straw: one at one end of our boxcar for the women and at the other end, a pile for the men to relieve themselves. Every couple of hours, when the train stopped, we'd push back the side doors of the cattle car and rush out into the fields, using them for toilets.

After about four days of traveling in this way, the train stopped abruptly. The guards opened the slatted doors of the cattle car and en masse we were pushed forward by those in back of us desperate to get off. We jumped into the unknown.

Adana, this is where we disembarked. When our train left, after disgorging its passengers, another arrived and many more Armenians were let out. Then, it too left and another would come, ad infinitum. There were now thousands of us following a couple of dozen heavily armed gendarmes who were Chechen guards wearing Turkish army uniforms. They were equipped with pistols, and whips were strapped to the sides of their horses, while cartridge belts were prominently wrapped around their waists. All had sabers. There were gendarmes also at the rear of our convoy.

We found out that we were at the southern end of the Cilician plain. It was near the town of Ceyhan, where we were finally allowed to rest. Exhausted, we brushed away the dozens of flies that had landed on our eyelids and filthy clothes. The bright sun was directly overhead and it was hot!

'Look over in that direction!' someone shouted. We turned and in the distance saw a castle at the top of a rocky mountain. It was Yilan Cale or Snake Castle, the castle of our Armenian king, Levon. Dead silence. All of us contemplated the significance of what we were seeing even in our pitifully destitute condition. However, I was absolutely beside myself with joy. It was true then what the storyteller had related to us back at the village, that many grand Armenian castles and fortresses dotted the landscape of Cilicia (or Lesser Armenia).

Here we were in the very same Cilicia. I even remembered some of the names of our famous castles and fortresses described by the storyteller: Sis, Silifke, Vahka, Baghras, Azgit, and Corycus. It was all too much. I thought my heart would burst from pride.

Thankfully, we were allowed to camp at the foot of the mountain. As far as I could see was an enormous detention camp of fellow Armenians. My father, with our family's help, set up our tent. We went inside, flopped down on the rock-hard ground, stomachs growling, and slept like the living dead.

I fell into a deep sleep and dreamt I was back in our village sitting directly across from the storyteller. He was telling a tale, and while I couldn't hear his words, his lips moved and his eyes were very expressive. I looked into his black eyes as the light of the kerosene lamp flickered. Suddenly I was whisked off to the entrance of a dark cave. I went inside and nearly tumbled head first as the ground was covered with large rocks and was unstable. I heard rustling and saw in terror a *vishap* or huge snake. This creature had the face and upper limbs of a man. Four smaller snakes moved stealthily nearby. The *vishap* spoke: "I'm hungry! Get me some food!" I was only too happy to oblige him, as I was starving. Since I was a hunter, I staked out a deer, killed it, and brought the animal back inside the cave whereupon I prepared it, taking the choicest pieces and jamming them onto a spit that I turned as I roasted the meat over a roaring fire. When the meat was cooked to perfection, the *vishap* and I ate until I thought my stomach would burst.

The *vishap* was so satisfied that he placed a stone with magical powers into my hand and told me to tell no one about him: not my mother, nor my father or brothers, as he was Shah-Mar, king of the snakes. He told me to come back and see him again, and next time to bring him some water. I replied, 'I will be back. I will come back . . .' and then I woke up.

It was very early. I awakened my mother and father and told them I was going to see Snake Castle up close. 'Don't stop me. I have to see it!' I said in a determined voice. My mother smiled at my courage, and looking through her bundle, found a piece of dried bread and stick of cured meat to take with me. 'Be careful!' my father entreated. 'Watch out for the gendarmes. They'll kill you without a second thought.' I told them I would pay attention. Then I stepped out of the tent and noticed no one was up and about as most people in our temporary tent city were sound asleep. Suddenly I saw a perfectly formed small stone on the ground and picked it up to take with me.

I headed in the direction of Snake Mountain and the legendary castle of our Armenian king, Levon. There was a soft, orange-yellow halo surrounding the deep lavender ruins of the castle in the early morning light. As I climbed upwards I saw that the lush grasses of the valley below were changing. The vegetation was stubbier with patches of thick berry bushes here and there. I stopped and picked off the choice plump fruit and stuffed them into my mouth, as I was very hungry. I walked higher and realized that this adventure was taking a lot longer than I had anticipated.

Closer now, I could see the well-built, semicircular towers and observed that the stone masonry of which the castle was constructed was in reality light gray in color, not lavender. I climbed on top of the parapet and walked along the edge that was at least three feet in width. Far below, I could see the tents of the deported Armenians.

Jumping off, I gingerly walked into the dark interior of one of the large rooms, passing through the arched doorway. 'Shah-Mar, your Excellency,' I shouted, 'I have returned as I promised!' No reply. I closed my eyes and listened for the rustling sound of snakes but could hear only my breath. Suddenly realizing how exhausted I was, I sat down in the dark room of the castle and took out the bread and cured meat my mother had given me. I ate slowly to make each morsel last longer, savoring each bite. Then I took out the perfectly formed smooth stone, rubbed it, and lay down, falling quickly to sleep.

I dreamt I was surrounded by dozens of little people, in royal dress, clamoring around my body to wake me up. I sat up and was stunned when I learned that one of them was none other than King Levon, accompanied by his retinue. The good king told me that his party was there to tend to my needs and make sure that I had plenty of food to eat. From another room of the castle, tiny servants with trays laden with wonderful roast lamb and pilaf, fruits, and pastries entered and encouraged me to eat whatever I wanted. I ate heartily and thanked them for their hospitality. Then, they were gone, and I woke up.

Strangely, I felt very satisfied, almost as if I had indeed finished a large meal. I looked out beyond the arched doorway and saw that it was growing dark. The castle was at the very top of a steep incline and surrounded by jagged rocks, which made it a perfect fortification for our king. I had to be careful, because climbing over those rocks would prove to be very precarious. Breaking my bones would add one more burden on my family. Secondly, my shoes had to last. I did not want to rip them up on those pointy rocks. 'Who knows how long the Turks are going to make us walk until we are relocated?' I thought.

I walked briskly down the side of the mountain to get back to my family. It was midnight when I snuck back into the tent so as not to wake up anybody. But they had all been waiting up for me.

My parents asked me if I had seen any snakes. 'No,' I replied, 'but there were plenty of berry bushes around the castle and the fruit was delicious!' I kept all my excellent adventures to myself.

After a few days of rest and uncertainty, the guards forced us to get up and continue walking. We went on to the town of Dort Yol, close to the Mediterranean Sea and far from Keramet and Lake Iznik. Many of our people were still carrying their bedding, while young children were holding onto their mother's hands. Babies were strapped to the backs of their mothers with fabric slings. Elders, barely able to move their arthritic limbs, were hobbling along as best as they could. All were frightened and exhausted from the journey.

The landscape began to change, and there were rumblings that we were no longer in Turkey proper but in the area of Syria. For three extremely hot days, we walked, and many people dropped dead in back of us and alongside. We wouldn't even turn to help anyone, so concerned were we with our own survival.

Near the town of Maskana, the Tigris became very wide and treacherous. I have no doubt that the gendarmes could have found a section of the river that would have made for easier crossing. But they didn't. Many were drowned here, including scores of children."

Towers of Snake Castle.

CHAPTER 4

OUR CONVOY
DECIMATED AND
WE REACH MOSUL

On the deportation route in Syria, Sarkis saw a small boy who had lost his mind, flaying his arms about and chirping like a bird.

RAQQA. "Even all these years later, the name sends a chill down my spine. The gendarmes were still guarding us, but now we were completely encircled by ferocious looking Arabs. I remember how terribly poor they appeared as they stared at our possessions, our children, and young women. Then, almost as if they responded to an invisible signal to attack, they let out blood-curdling cries and, lifting above their heads terrifying metal rods, they began hurriedly moving through our convoy and smashing our young and older men with these awful weapons. I could hear the cracks of human skulls as the tar balls at the ends of these rods met their marks. So many in our convoy were dead, and the dying were pleading for release, as they had horrendous wounds. Our women were in an absolute state of panic, rushing to the Arab women who were watching the event unfold, as were the gendarmes, like an audience in some kind of macabre theatrical engagement. Pleading to these women to please take their children, our Armenian matrons handed over their young ones to them. Worse was to come. Our adolescent girls and pretty young matrons who had lost their fathers, husbands, and brothers in this bloodbath were snatched and forcibly taken away. After this massacre, our guards, on horseback, prodded us with their sabers and yelled: '*Yalla! Giavurlar!*' ('Move on, infidels!')

Seeing an opportunity, Arab and Kurdish women from nearby villages would come after us and sell bread to those of us who had any money. So many in the convoy were dying or losing their minds. It was here that I observed a five- or six-year-old boy, arms outstretched, moving around in circles and chirping like a lost bird.

Sometimes, when it rained, a big puddle formed. The *Zaptiehs* (armed guards) would let their horses drink the water, and then the horses would defecate and urinate before we had a chance to drink the water ourselves. An adolescent girl saw that I was looking at her when she picked up some feces to eat but dropped it, shrugging her shoulders as if to say, 'What can I do?' Sadly, others ate the feces of the horses, and some even ate the feces of other people."

DEIR al-ZOR. "We camped here in tents, sleeping fitfully. While my family slept, I got up and walked outside. It was pitch black. There was heavy Turkish security around a mile-long trench. I could have been killed but I wanted to know about that mysterious trench. Somehow, I got past the sentries and witnessed, in horror, the enormous numbers of Armenian corpses piled into the trench. Turkish workmen were putting lime and then water over the corpses to make them decay faster. But not all were dead. I could hear the whimpering of those still alive. When I stumbled back into the tent and woke up my mother, she said later that I was babbling incoherently and she slapped my face to bring me back to my senses."

BETWEEN DEIR al-ZOR AND RAS al-AIN. "It was here that my father, Markar, lost the will to continue. He called us over to him and kissed us all good-bye, telling us, 'I'm finished!' That was all. He didn't say anything else. We left him sitting there in the desert. I would turn every few minutes and see his form becoming smaller and smaller as we walked on. Before this had taken place, my mother had given me coins to swallow one at a time. When I was able to crap out a coin, we would buy bread from Arab villagers. Mostly our 'diet' consisted of raw frogs, raw fish, turtles, and snakes."

RAS al-AIN. "This is where the gendarmes left us. There were so few of us remaining. Out of the thousands and thousands who had started the journey, a couple of hundred of us were barely alive. So much for the relocation for 'our own safety'!"

ZAKHO. "I reached the absolute end of my strength in Zakho, Iraq. I told my mother that I couldn't go on. We stayed here for a while: my mother, Nazar, Artin, and I. An Armenian by the name of Dr. Astarjian gave all of us food to help us stay alive. Then Nazar and Artin went on to Mosul."

MOSUL. "After resting for a few days and still under the care of Dr. Astarjian, Mother and I left Zakho and walked on to Mosul, a considerable distance away. Our shoes were in tatters, and our feet, bloated and bloody, were brownish purple in color. We were nearly nude and a pathetic sight. Mother said we needed to cover ourselves.

With the one gold lira we had left, Mother bought material, scissors, needle, and thread and made herself a dress: she also purchased pants for me to cover up my legs. She would then scrounge for food. One time, she found a discarded watermelon skin and hid it under her bodice as if it was a delicacy and shared it with me.

We were told that Armenian deportees were at Nebi Younis, and after asking how to get there, mother and I crossed the bridge close by. This bridge was made of air-filled animal hides. When we got to Nebi Younis, we saw that my brothers, Artin and Nazar, were there inside the large mud-walled enclosure that made up the famous ancient site. Younis is the name of the Biblical Jonah, and Nebi Younis was believed to have been Jonah's burial place. The bones of a large fish were also interred inside. Besides my brothers, there were a couple of hundred bedraggled Armenians who had survived the forced marches through the desert in Syria as we had.

Christian Arabs and Assyrians shared what little food they had with us. Not surprisingly, Turkish and German officers, who represented the countries responsible for the demise of our people throughout the Ottoman Empire, would walk through this enclosure and take whatever pretty girls and young women they wanted. A Turkish officer took Aghavni, a young matron from Keramet.

Nazar told my mother that he wanted to return to the Christian village of Tell Keif, where he thought he might have a better chance of surviving. We had passed the large village of Tell Keif on our way. More than anything, my mother wanted someone, anyone, from her family to survive, so she gave him her blessing. Then we all hugged and kissed him in farewell.

When he was gone, a group of Christians called *Nusrani* took all of us (two hundred or so) to their religious complex outside of Mosul. There were three big buildings. Every Saturday, people would come and sleep overnight after evening prayers. On Sunday, they worshipped in the Church of Saint Gurguis (a Chaldean Christian church). I remember there was a great deal of panic upon our arrival, as one of the worshippers said that he had seen a saint, depicted in a beautiful painting, literally step out of the frame. You would think that the worshippers would have cherished the idea of seeing a real live saint that they venerated. But no, they followed this hysterical man outside. Seeing a saint walking around would not have bothered me in the least, as I had seen so much already. While all of the worshippers were milling about outside, I rifled through their belongings and ate whatever food I could find. My mother spent a lot of time looking for me. When she found me, I told her that a saint had brought me bread and I shared it with her.

After this brief respite, Mother and I went back to Mosul. There was no one to look after us now. So we went from door to door, begging for food. This is how we lived for months. And then she was gone. I had been on one of my scavenging missions. When I came back to the place on the street, next to a building where we would sleep at night, I found that she had died. I knelt down to kiss her and, lifting up her listless arms, I wrapped them around my neck. I held onto her, rocking her back and forth, thinking that the warmth of my body would bring her back. But she was no more. I stood up and calmly informed an Arab nearby that my mother was dead and I could use some help. Sometime later, a cart and driver arrived and her body was taken away. The provisional government of Mosul hired people to pick up dead bodies and transport them to a common grave. That was her final resting place, Mosul, Iraq, so far from her beloved village of Keramet.

Now I was alone. My eyes were swollen and very painful whenever I closed them. I learned that other Armenian orphans like me were suffering from what was an epidemic of eye disease called trachoma. Three little Armenian children who were on the streets as I was became blind. I needed help, and fast.

I sat next to an elderly Arab man on the street. He looked at my eyes and shook his head in dismay. I kissed the old man's hand and asked him in Arabic, 'What kind of medicine is there for my eyes?' 'Go to the water buffalo people, called *Jamus*,' he replied. 'These people are known to be very honest, independent, kind, and tough minded.' He continued, 'Find a nursing mother who has a boy baby.' He told me what to say when I found her.

I did as he said and found a large woman with a friendly face holding a boy child. I went up to her and respectfully asked, '*Ibn?*' ('Boy?') She nodded, 'Yes!' I placed my forefinger up to my diseased red eyes and pointed to her large breasts and asked her to squirt some milk into both of my eyes. '*Haleeb! Haleeb!*' I repeated. She told me to kneel down and then she took a breast from underneath her *abaya* and, firmly pushing my head back, she squirted milk into both of my eyes.

The milk ran down my face and I lapped it up. She laughed and told me to see her the next day. I found an abandoned house and slept there all

night. In the morning, I rushed to the Tigris River to wash my eyes. I saw
her again and even went back a third day. I closed my eyelids and felt that
my eyes were better. I told my friends who had the same condition what
had happened. The good news is that many children did overcome this
dreaded disease and kept their eyesight.

My brother, Artin (aka Haroutiun), was at this time a slave in the home
of a very wealthy Arab by the name of Ahmed Beg. He was a widower
with six children, five sons and a daughter. The daughter's name was
Mezdia. Her brothers were Hussein, Sherif Beg, Abdul Rahman, Bekir,
and Mustafa. Artin told the family about me and they found something
for me to do. I would clean the house and care for the horses. My brother
and I slept in a small room on the roof of the house.

I liked Mezdia, Ahmed Beg's daughter. She was short and chubby, very
personable and talkative. She was fifteen years old and ran the household
with the help of a female servant. Mezdia and I talked together every day.
One of my jobs was to bring water daily (on the back of the donkey) to
the house. I would fill animal skins with water before loading them onto
the donkey. I complained to Mezdia that the work was too hard for me, so
I only had to do it for one week.

My clothes, as well as the clothes of my brother Artin, consisted of a
knee-length shift. No underwear, no shoes. We were barefoot. We hardly
ever bathed. When I ran my hand through my hair, it would come out in
clumps and then grow back again.

Artin and I were given a handful of bulgar wheat each day to eat.
However, I knew I would need money in the future, so I would steal grain
from the barn and sell it in the marketplace.

A year after I began working for Ahmed Beg, I was browsing in the
marketplace and looking through the piles of men's pants. I suddenly
spotted my father's pants. I was positive those pants were his. None of
the other pants in the pile had the distinctive color or were made of such
quality. I held onto this precious gift with one hand and with the other,
looked at my change and saw, to my dismay, that I did not have enough
money to buy them. I had only half of the price of the pants.

An acquaintance had been to Tell Keif and told us of the death of our brother, Nazar. The news hit us very hard. He was a golden-haired, handsome boy whom we loved so much. Now only two of us were left of our immediate family of seven souls.

A terrible episode took place in 1917. A female customer sat in a humble café that catered to common folk, and while eating the meal she ordered, came upon a tiny thumb complete with intact thumbnail. Horrified and disgusted, she took this thumb to the Turkish authorities. After investigation, it was discovered that the café owners, an Arab and his wife, had been kidnapping Armenian orphans, killing them, and cooking their remains in the stews that they served to their patrons. They were arrested, and their sentence was death by public hanging. I was in the huge crowd that witnessed the hanging in the city center of Mosul.

On October 30, 1918, Turkey sued for peace after being defeated in the First World War. While we Armenians and all of the other residents of Mosul were struggling to survive, the big powers were already at work carving up the lands of the Ottoman Empire. Early in November 1918, the British captured Mosul while we were there. A year later, in 1919, at the Paris Peace Conference, Iraq was formally made a Class A mandate entrusted to Great Britain. Palestine also was placed under British mandate and Syria was placed under French mandate.

During the First World War thousands more Assyrians and Armenians began to pour into Iraqi territory, seeking refuge from Turkish savagery. They came from the Hakkari Mountains in Turkey beyond Iraq's northern frontier and from the plains of Urmia in Iran. When a group of Armenians saw British soldiers on the streets of Mosul, they ran to them for help and some bread. They were brushed aside with the remark, 'We didn't come to Iraq to feed animals!'

Now that the British were there, members of the Armenian General Benevolent Union (AGBU) came to Mosul and went from door to door, looking for Armenian orphans and young matrons to rescue. I voluntarily left Ahmed Beg's home and went to the orphanage in Mosul. I wanted to be with Armenians. I was thirteen years old. I was given pants to cover my bare legs, a cotton shirt, and my head was shaved."

Nebi Younis (Jonah's tomb) goes back historically to the eighth century BCE. It is believed Jonah is buried there. In 1915, Armenians who survived the deportations to the deserts of Syria and Mesopotamia congregated in the courtyard of this sacred site. Photo by Eric Keast Burke, National Geographic, 1922. Permission granted to use. In public domain.

CHAPTER 5

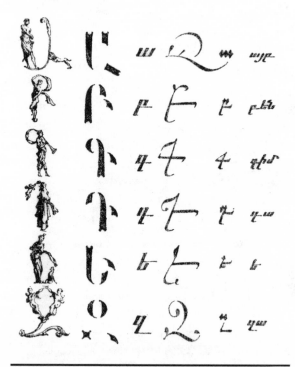

THE ORPHANAGE
AND MY FAVORITE
TEACHER, MIHRAN

The first six letters of the thirty-six letter Armenian alphabet created in AD 406 by the learned cleric Mesrop-Mashtotz.

"THE ORPHANAGE WAS MADE UP OF ONE BUILDING OF GOOD SIZE. It had two floors and many rooms. On the first floor, there was a kitchen and bedrooms. On the second floor, rooms were made available for both boys and girls. There were about three hundred children, among them more female orphans than male. Their ages ranged from the newborn to sixteen years. On the average, children stayed about one year. Many of the girls married Christian Arabs. Sometimes an Armenian man would come to select a girl for marriage. Small babies were taken to Baghdad where there was an orphanage capable of caring for infants.

The founder of our orphanage was the Armenian Archbishop Zaven Der Yeghiayan. Boghos Nubar Pasha, philanthropist and founder of the AGBU, provided funding for our orphanage. A group of ten children had a *mayrig* (a female caregiver) who supervised us. There was an Armenian guard posted at the door, but he did not carry a gun. Once in a while, the women who cared for us would wash our clothes.

There were two or three cooks. For breakfast, we were each given ten olives and a slice of bread, and for lunch the same. Dinner consisted of stews or soup. We took the pits from the olives and rubbed them against the rough walls. After we had flattened down the sides, we used a *mikhraz* (Arab word for awl) and bored holes in the flattened pits. We laced heavy string through the holes and created *tisbeks* (worry beads) and fingered them like the men did in our villages.

There were twenty of us per room. The rooms were smaller on the second floor. We slept on the floor and covered ourselves with burlap while sleeping. In the morning we lined up for exercise on the roof. Sometimes, during our one hour of exercise, we were allowed outside and we went running by the Tigris River. That was so wonderful! Once a month, we even bathed in the river.

There was no profiteering. If the people who worked in the orphanage had a family on the outside, perhaps a little food was taken home. I had fifteen gold pounds with me that I turned in to the orphanage when I moved in. They gave me my money when I left.

No girls were raped and no orphans were kidnapped. No children ran away. We had a few fights.

Our school was on the first floor. Everybody studied in the same room. The Armenian language was taught, reading and writing as well as mathematics. English was taught also, as Iraq at that time was under British control. No crafts were taught. We attended school four hours a day with one hour off for exercise.

All of us had to go to school. Armenian teachers taught all subjects. Mihran was my favorite teacher. He was from the town of Hadjin, where he had taught school. Our teachers were strict, and students were punished who talked back. When we entered school every morning, we sang this song while standing at attention. It began: 'Aravod loosoh, Arekagn artar, Ar ees looys dzakya.' This is from the famous hymn/chant Aravod Loosoh by Saint Nersess Shnorhali (1101–1171). It has thirty-six three-line stanzas, each starting with a letter of the then thirty-six-letter alphabet. The translation is: 'Morning of light, Righteous Sun, Shed your light on me.'

Once, in an assembly, one of the *mayrigs* sang a beautiful song by Gomidas Vartabed. She put a lot of feeling into it, and as she sang she looked skyward, as if calling to an imaginary bird flying overhead:

Groong, usdi gukas?

Dzara yem tzayneet

Groong, mer ashkharhen,

Khabrig muh chunees?

Translation:

Crane, where are you coming from?

I am a slave to your call

Crane, from my homeland,

Have you any news?

All of us in that auditorium cried at those words.

The entire time I spent in the orphanage, I knew I was learning how to read, and write, and do arithmetic, but in the back of my mind all I wanted was go back home to Keramet. There was a boy in the orphanage from a village near Lake Iznik. His name was Dikran. We shared our memories of the lake and our homes.

There were a few children who misbehaved, and they were punished. An adult would administer the punishment with a flexible stick. None of us worked for the orphanage, and none of us worked outside.

On holidays, we were given extra good food: pilaf and vegetables. I remember the Muslim holiday *Bayram*, which takes place after Ramadan. During Ramadan, Muslims fast, but after the fasting ends they celebrate with sweets. During this holiday, Mezdia visited me at the orphanage. She brought a large tray filled with a wonderful assortment of cookies and sweets. They were passed out to all of the children by the head cook. Mezdia also gave me a gift of ten silver *medjidie* (one is equal to eighty cents).

The Armenian Archbishop, Zaven Der Yeghiayan, occasionally visited our orphanage, as he lived in Mosul. I found out later that he was the Armenian patriarch of Constantinople in exile. On July 28, 1916, he had been deposed as patriarch by decree of the Young Turk government. This was done so our people had no one to turn to when they were experiencing the worst of the deportations and massacres. He had been transferred to Konia, then to Aleppo, then to Deir Zor, and finally taken to Mosul and liberated by the British in November of 1918. He returned to Constantinople on March 4, 1919, to resume his duties. When the Turks were victorious against the Greeks in 1922, he fled to Bulgaria and then onto Baghdad in 1924. He lived there until his death on June 4, 1947.

Every morning in the orphanage, we would pray. Once, we left the orphanage to attend a church service. I remember one orphan saying, 'I'm not Armenian. I'm *Pokhokagan!*' (Protestant).

In the area of hygiene, all of the boys had shaved heads. Some of the children had lice and trachoma. One child died in the orphanage, but I'm not sure what was the cause. The disease of *Tifo* (typhus) was widespread. In 1917, before I went into the orphanage, Turkish authorities inoculated everybody. I went and had an inoculation.

All these years later I remember my favorite teacher, Mihran, and the two math problems we had to solve in his class. Here is the first one. Three brothers went to a Turkish bath. The first brother asked: 'How much do I owe you?' The proprietor answered, 'Go to the cash register and see what's in there. Put that amount in and take forty cents out and go.' The second brother put thirty cents in and took forty cents out. The third brother did the same. After the third brother, there was no money left. How much money was in the cash register to begin with? Answer: There was thirty-five cents to begin with.

Here is another math problem to solve: 'I'm going to give you twenty lambs. You have to get rid of them in five days. You have to get rid of them in odd numbers.' Mihran promised that he would reward the problem solver with twenty-five cents. We worked on that problem all night. The next day, it was still not solved. I told the teacher when class started: 'If you solve the math problem, I'll give you fifty cents.' My classmates laughed uproariously and so did our teacher. I found out later that this problem has no solution.

There were children in the orphanage that could not speak, read, or write one word of Armenian when they entered. They certainly learned the language when they were there. Our teachers saw to that.

All of us knew what had happened to our people. The Turks had succeeded in totally destroying Armenian life and culture in Turkey that had been our home for over three thousand years. Not one of us had family photographs or any memorabilia of any kind. We all knew that we were orphans and realized that being in the orphanage was way better than being out on the street. We all helped one another, and most of us liked our adult supervisors. I remained there from November 1918 until May 1919, six months."

The Pitsak Gospel, an illuminated manuscript from the region of Cilicia, was created during the early years of the fourteenth century by the artist Sargis Pitsak, who enjoyed a great reputation in his time.

CHAPTER 6

I GO BACK
TO THE VILLAGE

The olive trees remained, and the Kerametsi villagers hoped that by harvesting and selling the olives it would keep them from starving.

"I DREAMT EVERY NIGHT ABOUT KERAMET. While in the orphanage I had learned that the Germans and their allies, the Austrians and the Turks, had been defeated in the First World War. A new Turkish government was formed, and we Armenians were given permission to return to our homes. I opted to stay where I was for the time being. The Armenian General Benevolent Union (AGBU) actively helped Armenians who wanted to return to their homes in Turkey. I found my brother in Mosul when I got out of the orphanage in May 1919. I told him that I wanted to return home, but he couldn't be bothered as he had an Armenian girlfriend, and that took precedence over anything else.

Aghavni Manougian, a fellow Kerametsi, who was twenty-eight years old, wanted to return also. She told me that after our family left the village, awful things happened. Turkish *chetes* (irregular forces) came to Keramet and began to round up the men. Her husband was one of them. They were separated from their families and taken out of the village some distance away, then made to dig their own graves. They were killed and thrown inside. Others were butchered with sabers, and still others were drowned in Lake Iznik. Aghavni had had four children: one son accidentally burned to death in boiling water used for laundry back in the village sometime before the massacres and deportations; an infant daughter, two weeks old, died during the deportations, as did another child who was four years of age. Only one child remained of Aghavni's family.

The route through Syria was particularly treacherous for Aghavni's convoy. Turkish irregulars following the Armenians prodded them with their bayonets so they would keep moving. They never let them rest. People were dying all around her.

Finally, they came to the bank of the Euphrates and Aghavni could see that the river was very wide and dangerous. Mothers with younger children tried to cross, but Aghavni saw that the current was bearing their children away to drown. She was absolutely desperate to save her last remaining child. A Kurdish woman, dressed all in black, looking to Aghavni like a phantom, was nearby. She rushed over to her, holding onto her daughter and telling her child how much she loved her and wanted her to live. Aghavni kissed her child over and over and then, speaking to the woman in Turkish, begged her to take her daughter and raise her. The woman showed great sympathy for Aghavni's plight and promised her that she would do as she was asked. That was the last Aghavni saw of her daughter, and in a state of mental and physical exhaustion she managed to swim across the Euphrates. The memory of her daughter would haunt her forever.

Twenty carriages arrived in Mosul, all paid for by the AGBU. Aghavni, a few other Armenians, and I boarded a carriage. The driver took us back through Syria to Deir al–Zor and on to Aleppo. In Aleppo, we boarded a train that took us through Turkey. The entire trip back was one of immense sadness. When we reached Constantinople, we paid for passage on a boat that took us to Yalova. In Yalova, we hired a driver who had an ox-driven cart and we told the driver to take us to Norkek. We slept in Norkek overnight.

The owner of the hostel where we stayed was an Armenian woman. I could tell she was going to say something rude to Aghavni by the way she was looking at her when Aghavni took out her purse, filled with coins, to pay for our rooms. 'How is it that you have so much money?' she asked, condescendingly, 'So many of our other girls were destitute.'

'Exactly what is the point you are trying so pitifully to make?' I asked, so furious now that it took everything I had to keep from slapping that hurtful woman across the mouth. 'I know what happened to our girls and women!' I shouted. 'Do you think in your wildest dreams they wanted the horrors that happened to them?' The proprietress of the hostel looked at the floor in shame, taking out a small handkerchief to wipe away a tear. Then, looking at Aghavni, she said, 'I'm very sorry about what happened to you.' Aghavni nodded.

We stayed at the hostel in two separate rooms. I hardly slept, anxious about what I was going to see the next day. How long had I dreamed of returning, and here I was at last so close to my home.

After a nice breakfast of cheese, bread, olives, and fruit, Aghavni and I began walking to Keramet. I could see the waterfalls coming out of the rocks and the rows and rows of our olive trees. Across the road, I saw the blue waters of Lake Iznik, where I had spent so many happy hours playing with my friends. My heart was beating so furiously I was afraid it would burst out of my chest. We went up the hill from the main road and I saw that our church, Saint Minas, was almost totally in ruins except for a small section in the back. Around the perimeter were large holes, which (I later learned) had been dug by Turks looking for the crosses and chalices of our church.

There were Turks standing around, looking darkly at us as we continued up the hill. Peeking out from the windows of homes previously owned by Armenians were Turkish women and children, looking to see who we were. As we both learned later, only about forty to forty-five of our villagers had returned from the hell of the deportations. Luckily for me, they included some of my relatives, my first cousins Armenouhi and Vartouhi and their husbands among them.

As I got closer to my family home, I heard a Turk shout, 'Better get out! Markar's son is back!' Someone hurriedly left the house.

The door was unlocked and I stepped into a totally empty shell. Where once it had been full of life, now there was absolutely nothing. I opened my mouth to call out for my mother and father and my brothers, hoping that by saying their names out loud I could conjure them up from the dead. But I was mute and instead went from room to room and reminded myself of the activities of my family.

We would sit on the floor here and eat our meals. Outside of this window was the pen where we kept the sheep, and alongside the pen was where the dogs stayed. There were no household items left. Everything had been taken. How I wanted to find a wooden spoon or bowl, my baby brother's sock, my mother's trousers, my father's fez. Nothing remained! Nothing!

I went upstairs, to the room where my mother and father slept, and got on my hands and knees looking for something, anything, that would remind me of them. Dust everywhere. My hands were covered with it. Then in that dust, I found a couple of strands of long, brown hair. Could they be my mother's, I wondered? I sat up and ran my fingers along the strands and caressed them and looked out the window at the high hills in the distance. This was all that was left of my mother besides my undying memories of her. I started to sob. It felt as if my tears would split my body in half. I collapsed onto the floor. But that only made it worse, because of my memories: my brother, Minas, on his way to join the army in Bursa; my father carrying the coffin of baby Bedros for burial; the desert, with my father sitting all alone; bringing Nazar his lunch in the hills where our sheep went to pasture; and then my mother caressing the watermelon skin on the street in Mosul. 'I love you!' I cried out. 'I love all of you!'

I don't know how long I remained there in that prone position, still crying. But in the early evening, I was rescued by Haji Muger, Armenouhi's husband. My relatives were growing concerned, and Haji came upstairs and found me. He picked me up off the floor, tenderly put his arms around me, and led me out of the house.

We were back home in Keramet, but how could we survive? All those who had helped to make our village functional and productive were either murdered or missing. We tried our best to return things to working order, thinking that our ancient olive trees would help keep us alive. So we worked in the orchards.

As I spoke with my relatives, I found out what they had gone through during the deportations. They concurred that most of the able-bodied men had been killed outright within two or three days after the notice for the deportation had been posted. All had lost family members, by murder, starvation, or disease. My brother's fiancée, Ariknazan, was taken by an Arab in the wastelands of Syria never to be seen again. My beautiful blonde cousin Armenouhi and her equally beautiful black-haired sister Vartouhi were taken by Chechens and in 1918 rescued. When freed, they sent a man to get their brother, Merger, out of Mosul and back to Keramet.

Merger rescued a beautiful orphaned girl, Turvanda, alone on a road, who had been kidnapped by the Turks during the deportations. Heaven knows what she had experienced. He married her in Tekirda (near the border with Greece). Now both he and his beautiful blonde wife, Turvanda, were also in Keramet. Yaghanegi Minas also had come back to the village. He had been a soldier in the Turkish army. But he didn't stay long in Keramet. He left and went to Rushjuk, Bulgaria.

Aghavni opted not to stay in Keramet and went to Constantinople, where she obtained a position caring for orphans. She remarried a Minas Pashayan, who had two children. Her husband died tragically six months later, after having been shot by an Armenian male over a ridiculous misunderstanding. He had been shot with dum dum bullets in the leg. The injury, although not life-threatening at the time of the shooting, became infected, and he died as a result. In 1921 Aghavni was able to immigrate to America. In New York, she married Artin Dirtadian and gave birth to two daughters, Florence and Rose.

My cousin Armenouhi's husband, Haji Muger, was an interesting character. He never referred to himself as an Armenian. Was it self-hatred or disappointment about what had happened to our people? He always referred to himself as a Turk. Vartouhi was married to Hagop Peselian and they had a son. Besides Merger and his wife, Turvanda, my other cousins were also there: the brothers Zaren, Krikor, and Stepan.

We picked olives from the trees when it was harvest time, and Turks from surrounding Turkish villages came and helped us. Life went on. I fell once and broke my arm. A villager set it, and not very well, as my arm at the elbow is still crooked.

Once I saw a large, black bear on the road as I was working alone in the olive grove. I remained very still until he was gone, and then I ran out of there. Many animals could be found near the village: rabbits, squirrels, wild pigs, foxes, and, as I mentioned, bear.

I was back in my beloved village of Keramet, but I did not feel safe at all. Everything was very different, and for good reason. Brigands, thieves, and murderers controlled all roads. Young boys such as myself were especially vulnerable to kidnapping, torture, rape, and brutal murder. We were already aware of three pitiful deaths. Lawlessness was the order of the day.

My cousin Zaren was not going to stand idly by while all of this was going on. The Turkish villagers of Chakurlu (now Cakur) that had been so close and friendly to us before 1915 were sadly behind many of the atrocities. While the Peace Conference was meeting in Paris to negotiate the World War I settlement, Greece invaded Turkey on May 15, 1919. As soon as Zaren heard invading Greek forces were arriving in the southern Marmara region, he sought them out for retaliation purposes. Zaren took them to Chakurlu and pointed out to the Greeks those responsible for the killings of the Armenian boys. The killers were taken away and we never saw them again.

During this period of severe hardship, all of us were needed to keep the village functioning. So, I had to put aside my desire to leave and join the Greek army not because I wanted to turn into a killer but because I felt it would be safer to be a soldier. But I stayed and helped in the orchards from May through September 1919. The Greeks had already taken command of Bursa on July 8, 1919.

Before I left, at the end of September, I sat down with my relatives and told them of my plan. They understood that I had every reason to want to join the Greek army, as they also were frightened. There was no way, they continued, that they could keep me from harm. There were so few of us taking care of such a large village, and we were so spread out while carrying out our tasks.

At the conclusion of our meeting, we all stood up and bowed our heads in prayer while my cousin Merger said a few words, blessing my journey. When we opened our eyes, some tearfully, I knew I was ready. But who would believe me if I claimed to be old enough to enlist, as my face was as smooth as a baby's? Looking around, I found a piece of charcoal and rubbed it on my upper lip and cheeks.

When my relatives saw me, they said that, truly, I looked older and tougher than my fourteen years. They also said that, if things grew worse, to look for them in the Armenian Church in Tekirdag, near the border between Turkey and Bulgaria, when my tour of duty was over. I walked away from Keramet for the last time, headed for Bursa and the Greek encampment.

During the period before the massacres and deportations of our people, there were events in Keramet that I had no knowledge of because of my youth. The elders of the village were not going to take me into their confidence and relate critical information. I feel it is important to explain the circumstances leading up to the burial of our village treasures and other unforeseen events that transpired while I was a soldier in the Greek army. For this information, excerpts from the memoir of another Kerametsi, Hagop Nigogossian, are necessary to round out the history of our village during these treacherous times. My own experiences will continue after this chapter."

CHAPTER 7

FROM THE MEMOIR
OF KERAMETSI
HAGOP NIGOGOSSIAN

The day Hagop Nigogossian left Bolis (Istanbul) Central Prison, 1929.

Excerpt from "Memoirs of My Exile 1915–1929" by Hagop Nigogossian

"IN 1915, THOSE OF US NOT KILLED OUTRIGHT WERE DEPORTED. We were with my father-in-law, our archpriest Tomas Khengigian, until Qatma, in Syria where he died. Then we continued walking with our archdeacon, Sarkis Gugherian, until Ras al-Ain. At night, we pitched our tents next to each other. Our archdeacon had contracted cholera and was very ill. He called us over to his tent and gave us the following information before passing away: 'I have no hope of recovery. You, Hagop, have a good chance of staying alive, so I need to tell you something, something that I had promised Tomas that I would not tell a single soul. Sometime before the deportations, Tomas and I buried the crosses. I'll tell you now where they are, so if you are able to return to Keramet, you may take them out and rebuild the church. Only our priest Tomas knew this, and he made me promise not to reveal the secret to anyone. My oath to him ends here!' After a few days, we buried him along with many, many others.

In late 1918, when we were allowed to come back to our villages, I returned. It was night. I walked up the hill and saw that most of the church had been destroyed almost down to its foundation. I saw that the room behind the altar was still intact. None of our villagers knew the whereabouts of the crosses, although they had surmised that our priest had buried them someplace.

I should tell you now about someone who played an important part in this story. My cousin, Semerji Bedros, who was older than I, absolutely adored the church. Before the deportations and during the tabernacle feast days, he used to take a break from his work to decorate the main altar and the two altars adjacent to it. I always thought of him as a faithful and trustworthy person. It was for that reason that I took him to the church the day after I returned. We found the crosses buried underneath the heavy stone that had been used to conceal them. We did not remove them because we felt they were in a very safe place.

There was no viable government or authority, and therefore our village and surrounding villages, with what was left of the Armenians, was in a very precarious position. So, if the Turks knew about the crosses, they would have come into our village and taken them away, with no questions asked. There was so much robbery and looting going on all around the countryside. It was total chaos!

For that reason, we decided not to reveal the hiding place until some semblance of authority had been restored. Two weeks went by, and my cousin was becoming anxious to see if the crosses were still there. Without telling me, he took a break from his work and went back to the church to the room in which they were buried. I know his intentions were good. He was just curious.

He removed the big stone with great difficulty and dug frantically, using only his hands. At first he saw a small piece of wood. He dug deeper and found that it was part of the box containing the holy oil. Bedros breathed a sigh of relief, knowing that the treasure was still there. However, when he tried to put back the large stone cover, he couldn't return it to its original place and left in dismay. He was agitated and thought that because of his actions the crosses would be revealed.

Immediately Bedros went to the elders and told them that he had a premonition that the crosses were going to be stolen and therefore he went to the church and saw that, yes, the stone cover had been displaced. The village elders believed him. They went with him to the church, removed the crosses and chalices, and brought them to Tertsagian's home.

The day that all of this transpired, I was out fishing with friends at Lake Iznik. When we were on our way back home, villagers came up to us and told us the great news that the crosses had been found. Immediately I knew that Bedros had stupidly revealed the hiding place. I was very angry as I made my way to Tertsagian's home. Going up the stairs, I saw Bedros. He tried to convince me that he was innocent by telling me the same story he had told the others. If it hadn't been for the fact that Bedros was older than I, I would have slapped him then and there. I had always respected him until this incident.

I went into the house and saw that all of the members of the Board of Trustees of the church were seated. I greeted them and sat down. 'I see,' I said, 'all of you are happy having found the valuables of the church, and you should be. But I am sad because I'm thinking that we will lose these items. Look around you. We have no security in our country. The Turks can very easily come and take everything without even using their guns. We have no arms with which to defend ourselves.'

I turned to Bedros who was shaking. The poor man was afraid of his own shadow. I asked him: 'Do you have a way to save these crosses?' He shrugged helplessly. I then looked at the others: 'What do you think? How can we save them? We can't postpone the matter any longer. We have to act immediately!' None of them could offer a practical solution. So I had to take care of it.

'Listen,' I said, 'tomorrow, I will put two boxes on my horse and ride over to Gemlik. I'll stay there for a few days, and that's when you will start a rumor in the village that I have taken the crosses to the residence of the patriarch. This way the issue will be solved. But you will have to keep this a secret and not even tell anyone, even members of your own family. As for the crosses and other valuables, we'll place them in a box and seal it with the stamp and notarization of the head of our village and the signatures of our Board of Trustees. We'll prepare three copies. One will stay with whomever is keeping the valuables, the other copy stays with our village head man and the third one will be kept by one of the members of the Board of Trustees.'

I then said that someone among us should take responsibility for keeping the crosses and for telling someone close to him where they were. The fewer who know about the valuables, the less likely will be the risk that they will be stolen. Then the issue of choosing someone came up. They all pointed to me, and in unison said that I was the only trustworthy person among them. After the official signing, they all left. I remained with the owner of the house, my cousin Tertsagian. I knew he wasn't very trustworthy, but at this point there wasn't much I could do. I couldn't take them home. I was looking after my niece and I didn't want people to harass her in my absence, looking for the treasure. The valuables would have to be buried at my cousin's home. I warned him that if this treasure were lost, they would be lost also. My cousin, his wife, and I were the only ones who knew where they were. Little did I realize then that, when I was incarcerated two months later for an unrelated reason, my cousin's wife would take two of the crosses to Constantinople and sell them.

The next day, I placed the empty boxes on my horse and went to Gemlik. I stayed there for four days and then came back to the village. My actions had convinced the villagers that the valuables had been taken to the Patriarchate for safe keeping.

When I was imprisoned sometime later, men from the Turkish village of Meligee attacked our village. All of the people who remained in Keramet ran away as the Turks set fire to the village. The house where the crosses were buried was burned down.

When the Greeks, in 1919, got the upper hand, the residents of our village, including my cousin Tertsagian, returned to Keramet. The crosses were taken out of the ground where they had been buried and brought to Gamarag. When the

Greek army was defeated, the Kerametsis, in Gamarag, went on to Rodosto, and then into Bulgaria. There our villagers handed the crosses over to the Bulgarian church authorities in Varna, to relieve themselves of the burden of caring for them.

It was only in 1957 that I sat down and wrote a letter to one of our villagers, Hagop Saredayan, to see if he could track down our crosses in Varna. I told him to make sure that the church elders in Varna included in their records the fact that the crosses and chalices brought to them years earlier had come from the village of Keramet and mentioned the names of our archpriest and the archdeacon. Sadly, no evidence of these crosses or chalices of Keramet could be found in Varna. That part of the tale ends here. At least we kept them out of the hands of the Turks.

During the deportations, our village of Keramet, compared to the neighboring Armenian villages, had been impacted the most. Before the massacres and deportations there were 1,200 or so residents in the village, but barely forty to forty-five returned. All were in pitiful condition. We were hoping that our lives would improve with the harvesting of the olives. When I came back, there were Turks who were not members of our original village living there, but gradually they went back to their own villages.

In August 1919, one of the organizers of the Armenian Revolutionary Federation (ARF) by the name of Aram Varantian came to our village while on tour of the area. He stayed in my home for two days, after which he went to Soloz and Gurle. He wanted our village of Keramet to establish an ARF chapter. I told him all well and good, but we had other important priorities, namely to clothe and feed ourselves. Why put such a burden on men who are starving? He kept the pressure on, and I told him finally that in a few months, after the olives had been harvested and sold, we would then do as he insisted. Unfortunately, this was not to be, as twelve of our fellow villagers, including myself, would be out of the picture. Years later, I saw this same Aram Varantian during the Second World War in Paris.

At the end of September 1919, a group of thirty Armenians came to our village. These were young men who were seeking retaliation against the Turks for the deportations and atrocities committed during the war and who had nothing to lose because they had already lost everything. They arrived at night and needed a place to rest until the next day, when they planned to go to the very wealthy Turkish village of Boyaleja (now Boyalica). This Turkish village was approximately one-and-a-half hours away from Keramet. Their plan was to destroy that village.

When they arrived that night, I was standing guard. The two other men who were supposed to do guard duty were absent. I saw in the dark, at the far end of the village, a group of these men seated in front of a house, resting. I recognized two of them. They were sitting in a place too noticeable and therefore not safe. I pointed out a nearby home and told them to go inside, where I joined them. Then they revealed their plan to me and asked my opinion. I said, 'Your plan will put you in great danger; I know that Boyaleja is a wealthy village, but even if you succeed in stealing their wealth, you could lose a great deal.' Before I had finished speaking, one of the men who was probably their leader and was seated next to me took me aside. He pleaded, 'I beg you, don't discourage them because on our way here, all they wanted to do was abandon the plan and go back home. In this case, it's better not to think too much about the details.' I grew even more skeptical after hearing that.

They left the next day and arrived at the Turkish village at sunset while all of the men were at prayer. All this I found out later. They had wanted to surround the café, which was next to the mosque. But after being confronted by the patrons of the café, they ended up accosting the Muslims in the mosque and seized more than thirty of them. The Armenians were extremely nervous. When one of their men was hit by friendly fire and killed, they panicked and forced the thirty Turks to leave the village with them.

On the outskirts of the village, the Armenians lined up the hostages and ended up killing sixteen and wounding the others, who ran off. The Armenians left immediately afterwards, in order to avoid the arrival of the Turkish police from Nicaea, who would assist the villagers of Boyaleja. The Armenians disappeared. Even though they could have taken better advantage of the hostage situation, they did not. This whole misguided 'adventure' was total nonsense and complete idiocy. We Kerametsis paid the ultimate price.

On October 16, 1919, a group of policemen arrived at Keramet and surrounded the café. This was fifteen days after the incident at Boyaleja. The commander took a piece of paper out of his pocket and read a list of twelve names. I was on the list. We were all under arrest. Those who were present and on the list were taken to the nearby village of Chakurlu. It was obvious that this action by the police was premeditated. They knew very well that no one in our village was responsible for the incident at Boyaleja. They couldn't find the Armenian brigands who had killed and wounded the Turks, so they went after us. The old expression fits well here: 'When the Turk doesn't reach his camel, he hits its back!'

When we arrived at Chakurlu (now Cakur), canes made of strong branches of a tree had already been prepared. They took us out one at a time and beat us. It was obvious that they were retaliating, because we were not interrogated about the incident that had precipitated our arrest. The next day, we were taken to the spot where the bodies of the murdered Turks had been found and we were beaten terribly, and then sodomized in full view of bystanders. These same bystanders recognized us as being from Keramet and not guilty of those murders, but they just stood and watched.

The policemen had come to an agreement with the Turkish villagers to fabricate a story that the perpetrators were Kerametsis. From Chakurlu, we were taken to Iznik, where we were impounded for nineteen days. My weak vocabulary cannot describe the tortures we were subjected to on our way there. Our bodies were no longer flesh colored, so covered were we with black-and-blue marks and bloodied.

Before handing us over to the government, we were taken around Iznik and shown to the population, who were told that we were the ones who had invaded the Turkish village, killing and wounding the worshippers. The Turkish commander sitting astride his horse led us. We stumbled behind him as we were tied together with heavy ropes and flanked by police.

We were imprisoned for nineteen days in Iznik in a very small room where normally only two people would fit. The government sent out notices announcing to the gullible population that the thieves and murderers had been arrested. Finally those who had been wounded in the raid by the Armenian brigands came to identify us. None of them recognized that we were the perpetrators, and yet they all, without exception, bore false witness against us, pointing to one or another of us as being involved in the 'robbery.'

Even though we were incarcerated and had no access to the outside, whenever a robbery of any kind occurred, we were accused of having been involved. Guards wouldn't leave us alone day or night. So-called witnesses would come to insult and slap us and at night we were once again sodomized and tortured by the guards.

On the twentieth day, we were taken to Nicomedia (now Izmit) for the trial. The policemen who were taking us beat and tortured us to a point where we were physically unrecognizable.

It was night when we arrived at Yalakdere (an Armenian village). After half an hour, they took us to Chamourlu Bayer Boshnak village. We stayed there overnight. The next day, we arrived at Kara Mosul (now Karamursel) and the policemen handed us over to those overseeing the police station and left. That same night we were beaten and tortured horribly. This was to be our last torture. After a while, we were taken, by boat, from Constantinople to Nicomedia and put in jail there. Inside, we were surrounded by Armenian inmates shocked at our appearance and [who] wanted to know what had happened. We told them the whole story.

We collapsed in a corner and slept until the next day. We were awakened and taken into a room where a nicely dressed man by the name of Maksoud Gdavjian told us not to worry, adding that everything would be done to set us free. Our prelate, Archbishop Stepannos, hearing of our arrival at Izmit, had specifically sent Mr. Maksoud to encourage us. We were given olives, cheese, bread, and a big pot of meat soup. For one solid week, he visited us and brought us food until we told him that we would be taken care of by our families. After two weeks, the Archbishop visited in person. He said that he would get us out with dignity. With him were two attorneys: a Turkish citizen and Souren Effendi from Constantinople.

On our trial date, no witnesses showed up from Boyaleja village because they knew that we were not the guilty ones. They had been following instructions from the police chief to witness falsely against us. I remember one of the witnesses saying: 'My lord, why should I sin. I don't recognize any of these men. I gave a statement before, but I was obliged to do so!'

The actions of that group of Armenian brigands had been a disaster for us. And yet, even though we were not guilty in the least, we received life sentences. Archbishop Stepannos followed our case and asked the court to cut our sentences in half.

The political situation in Turkey at that time was dire. We had been transported to Constantinople because Izmit was the front line during the war between the Greeks and Turks. When the Turks withdrew from their front lines, the Kerametsis moved to Gemlik. After the Kemalist victory, the Kerametsis left Gemlik and went to Salonika and from there to Rodosto with Archbishop Stepannos and afterwards to Bulgaria.

While the population of southern Marmara was in flux, we twelve remained incarcerated. I would like now to share with you their names: Sumerji Bedors (my cousin), who couldn't harm an ant and who had discovered the crosses; Krikor Haji Torrosian; Alexan Zeliflian; Hovagim Khorokian; Garabed Vartanian; and Mugerditch Karanfilian. These men were set free with no charges against them. However, the rest of us served time: Hagop Vartanian (who was Garabed's older brother); Hagop Karanfilian (who was Mugerditch's younger brother); Stepan Garabedian (who was Deli Sarkis's first cousin and who, according to Sarkis, was so gentle, he couldn't hurt a fly); Zadik Rupenian; Madat Hagopian; and myself.

I was able later to find out what happened to some of them. Garabed Vartanian, while going from Yayla Kova to Chengiler, with his friends, fell victim to a trap set by villagers from Meligee. They died after being tortured to death. Bedros was killed in Lebanon but I don't know the circumstances.

The six of us serving time were alive in 1957. But, then, as if by agreement, three passed away one after another within three months of one another. First, Stepan Garabedian passed away in Bulgaria; Hagop Vartanian died in Constantinople; and Madat Hagopian died in Armenia.

My beloved friends, we all suffered ten years of vile barbarities in prison for crimes we never committed. We drank together from the bitter cup. How painful it is that your tombs are miles away and I will never be able to pay my respects.

Forgive me! My beloved friends, *hoghe tetev ka*! ('Let the soil be light on you.') Sleep in your eternal rest with no worries, knowing that Turkish atrocities do not work in eternity.

I was set free on October 22, 1929, after serving for ten years and six days. In June 1930 I caught a ship to Marseilles, keeping my citizenship papers (thinking that being a Turkish citizen might be useful one day). However, I would never return to the hellish circus of Turkey again."

CHAPTER 8

THE GREEK ARMY
AND THE HORROR
OF SMYRNA

Bursa, Turkey, 1921. Sarkis on left and Garabed (born in Norkek) on right in the Greek army. Garabed was a brave soldier. The words on the banner behind them read: "Remembrance of Proussa this too shall pass." Below the words is the double headed eagle, symbol of the Byzantine Empire.

"IT WAS LATE IN SEPTEMBER 1919 WHEN I DECIDED TO LEAVE THE VILLAGE. Minas Peeligian and some others had already taken the sacred vessels and crosses of our church, Saint Minas to Varna, Bulgaria. I have no doubt that if I had stayed on, and not gone off to join the Greeks, I would have become the thirteenth victim of Turkish injustice. I learned later that twelve of our men and boys had been arrested in early October. Walking to the city of Bursa would take me more than one day. So, I decided to stay overnight in a hostel that was owned by a Turk and his helper. I ate and slept there.

When I got to Bursa, Greek soldiers were everywhere. There were also Armenian boys who had come back, having survived the massacres and deportations. They were from the villages of Norkek, Chengiler, Jarah, and Yenijeh. After speaking with them, I learned that at the end of the First World War, the Allies were going to give Konya to the Italians, and the English sanctioned the Greek plan to invade Anatolia, which the Greeks did in May 1919, killing many Turks. The Greeks came to Bursa by way of Mudanya, and instead of fanning out all over the region, they hunkered down in Smyrna and then later in Bursa. This was before the Greek army advanced inland and into the trap set by Mustafa Kemal (Ataturk), leader of the Turkish nationalist forces. Because of this misguided adventure, many Greeks, in their villages, had been killed.

I went to the army camp outside of the city of Bursa. When the young soldier in charge of giving out uniforms and boots asked me my name, I replied that it was 'Deli Sarkis' (Crazy Sarkis)! Boy, he thought that was funny. My paternal grandfather was called 'Deli Sarkis,' a man noted for his fearless reputation and for being an outspoken defender of the honor of his family and of the downtrodden. I thought that by taking on his moniker 'Deli,' some of his bravery would rub off on me. It was very nice to get the new uniform and those boots after being in rags for so long.

I was in the midst of a couple of hundred men and boys while Sergeant Vangelis oversaw our training. He was fair minded, but also a strict disciplinarian. He had so little time to make soldiers out of this disorganized group of young men. Our training lasted one month and consisted of calisthenics, running, and practicing on targets. We ate communally. Once we learned how to use rifles, which I did well as I had a steady hand and very good eyesight, three or four of us Armenian boys would leave the encampment at night. Unbeknownst to the staff, we would hunt down Turkish males and kill them.

We fought in some front-line combat against the Turks. It was then that I captured a Turkish scout, and while involved in that action, I noticed a huge enemy advance prior to an attack. It's a good thing, too, as the battle that ensued was won by the Greeks at a cost of 250 Turkish lives. I received a battlefield promotion to corporal. I knew Grandfather would have been proud.

In 1921, Haroutiun Taghtajian, the brother of my brother's fiancée, came to our encampment. His father, Krikor Haroutiun Taghtajian, had been the bookkeeper of the village. Haroutiun had lost nearly all of his family during the massacres and deportations, and he was filled with rage. From his pocket he took out lots of money and bought a machine gun from the Greeks. Curious as to what he planned to do with it, I followed him as he carried the machine gun to a hill outside of the city. There were scores of people milling about. He turned his sights on them and opened fire, killing many bystanders. Soon after that incident, he left Turkey and went to Plovdiv, Bulgaria, where he eventually married. He died at a young age.

One day in 1921 a Greek photographer came to our camp and took pictures. I had two pictures taken: one where I'm standing next to a very brave Armenian soldier, Garabed, from Norkek, and the other of myself holding a rifle, squatting on one knee and battlefield ready.

In November of the same year, after a year and a half in the Greek army, I decided not to rejoin and received an honorable discharge. I very much admired Sergeant Vangelis and many of the Greek and Armenian soldiers I encountered during my service, but I was skeptical about the Greek army's plan in Turkey. Moving on, I boarded a boat in Mudanya and arrived in Smyrna, a city with a huge Greek and large Armenian population. It was at night when I arrived, so I stayed in a hostel called Shayan Khan across the street from the Armenian Church.

The next day, I ran into my friend Dikran Nahabedian in a café nearby. He originally had been from the village of Karsak, across the lake from Keramet. We spent some time in Smyrna going to the quay and looking at the smartly dressed men in straw hats and the elegantly dressed women carrying parasols. The beautiful blue water was lapping the quay. We even visited the Armenian Church. It was a crystal clear day.

Dikran told me that he had a job picking grapes on a farm in the nearby village of Chobanisa. We went and stayed a short while but decided to leave and went on to Manisa. Before the deportations, Manisa had a considerable population of Armenians. We found work on a farm owned by an Armenian and then met another Armenian boy by the name of Bedros Inejian working there. The three of us worked hard for a number of months and enjoyed the camaraderie, the pay, and the outdoors. This lasted until the day that while in the fields we saw in the distance thousands of Greek soldiers heading our way. Realizing in horror that they were in retreat, we panicked and hurriedly rushed to the train station. We caught a train that was heading toward Smyrna, thinking we would be safe there. It was September 1922.

When the train stopped in Smyrna, we got off and scrambled to the Armenian prelacy complex. On our way there, we saw Mustapha Kemal in a flashy car surrounded by his officers. Squeezed in between the officers was a stern-faced woman wearing a hat and matching coat trimmed with a fur collar. I found out later that this was Halide Edib, Mustapha Kemal's associate.

When we arrived, the churchyard of Saint Stephen was overflowing with Armenians who had locked up their homes and had come to take refuge there. Every inch of the place, from the courtyard to the church and adjoining rooms, was filled with people. We also found out, after talking with them, that tens of thousands of Greek and Armenian refugees were streaming into Smyrna from surrounding towns and villages. They were following the retreating Greek army. Transport ships were removing as many of the Greek soldiers as possible from Smyrna, but no refugees were taken on board. The city's gendarmes were also leaving. No police or civil guard would remain to protect the people who were left. On top of that, the first battalion of Mustapha Kemal's army was approaching, and that caused near panic in the prelacy compound.

On Sunday, September 10, 1922, no church bells rang out from Saint Stephen. We heard Turkish soldiers taking up positions outside the prelacy compound, threatening us, firing their guns, and running about outside the complex in order to set up their positions. We knew what was going on outside because we had placed mirrors against the corner windows of the building. We saw that the Turks were breaking into homes and taking young girls to nearby abandoned buildings, never to be seen again.

The leader of our group, Garabed Chavoush, saw to it that rifles and pistols were distributed, along with available ammunition, to those of us who knew how to use guns. He also divided us into shifts for guard duty so we were able to sleep for a few hours. Suddenly we heard the Turks speaking loudly in English, telling us that they were there to liberate and defend us and calling upon us to open the door. Garabed ordered us to take our positions behind windows and furniture and be ready to fire in case we were attacked.

After their entreaties, the Turkish soldiers lobbed grenades into the courtyard. The grenades exploded, killing and maiming people. A horse was killed. We began firing on the Turks from our positions. The Turkish troops then turned their machine guns on the prelacy, shattering windows all around us and killing many more. Screaming and moaning could be heard everywhere. Garabed then told us to fire, one shot after another, to show our strength to the Turks. We did. There was no response from outside. We were then able to tend to the wounded.

Food was distributed but none of us felt like eating. Sanitary conditions were becoming deplorable inside the prelacy, and many of us were talking about taking our chances on the outside, which meant it was time to negotiate with the Turks.

A few days later, an Italian Catholic priest, named Don Scaliarini, visited the prelacy, telling us that he had been in talks with the Turkish military and had secured permission to guide everyone to the quayside under the protection of twelve French sailors. The one condition was that we would have to leave our weapons behind, and all of us would be subject to inspection as we left the building.

My friends and I immediately took what money we had and slipped it in our shoes. Dikran, Bedros, and I were roughly frisked and searched by the Turkish soldiers as we left. Once we were outside the prelacy, we saw all around us roving bands of irregulars loitering and demanding valuables and young girls.

The three of us moved fast and left the group. We hid in an abandoned building. We remained inside for a couple of days. We had absolutely no food or water, so in desperation we decided to make a run for it and head for the quay. What a mistake! Turkish soldiers were in control of everything. There was such a commotion that I lost sight of Dikran and Bedros. A Turkish soldier grabbed me by the back of my jacket, pushing me so hard that I stumbled. Along with two hundred Greek and a lesser number of Armenian boys and men, we were herded into the Basmakhanien Station. Then we were hurriedly lined up against a wall and quickly the machine guns were set up and turned on us. When the guns began firing, I thought to myself, 'This is it!' I heard the rat-ta-ta-tat of the guns, and as I saw boys falling all around me, I fainted.

Sometime later, I woke up. I looked around. Dozens of bodies were lying in all kinds of positions. Blood was everywhere: on faces, arms, and legs, evidence of terrible wounds. A young man, next to me, pleaded aloud for someone to finish him off. His legs were a bloody pulp. My forehead and right leg were throbbing. I saw vague shapes that were khaki uniformed soldiers. 'Lay still!' I thought to myself. 'The murderers are still here!'

Turkish soldiers stepped on top of the bodies to better position their fixed bayonets and they thrust the blades forcefully into those still alive. I surmised that a bayonet was the origin of my wounds and had glanced off my skull but penetrated my leg. There were crunching sounds of blade crushing bone, splattering flesh and moans, and then silence. The not-so-vague shapes left. Their work was done. I leapt up, but lightheaded, I fell back down. I desperately managed to climb over the bodies of the dead until I reached a clearing and then made a run for what I surmised was the direction of the quay.

Everywhere I looked, behind me, to the left and right, buildings were on fire. I saw sheets of flame and buildings crashing down, while the heat felt as if it was searing my skin. I learned later that Turkish soldiers had set fire to Smyrna, targeting the Armenian section first. The flames quickly spread, and soon the entire city except for the Turkish section was aflame.

Then, mysteriously, through the smoke, I saw what looked like two little ghosts. I stumbled forward and there were two little girls, their once white pinafores bloodied and covered with soot, and their braids undone, and dark hair streaming down their backs. One was about seven years old and the other appeared to be a couple of years older. They began screaming when they saw me stumbling forward, terrified at my bloodied appearance.

'I'm not going to hurt you, girls. I'm not a Turk!' I exclaimed, forcefully. 'For goodness sake, where are your parents?' Then, together sobbing, they blurted out that they were from Manisa and with their parents they left their home and followed the retreating Greek army to Smyrna, thinking they would be safe here. A sword-wielding Turkish soldier had killed their parents and took whatever they had of value on their clothes and bodies. The soldier began moving toward the girls, when, luckily for them, his attention was diverted by another unarmed family, and that's why they were able to get away. My heart rose up in my throat as I thought of all the lost girls of my village. I grabbed their little hands and yelled out: 'I'm going to save you. Trust me. Do whatever I say. Understand?' They both nodded. 'Now, we're going to run as fast as we can to the quay!' We ran without stopping, focused entirely on what lay ahead.

When we reached the quayside, named Cordon Boyee, I couldn't believe my eyes. There were so many terrified people crammed into that small space. Much later I was told that a half million people had been packed into an area a mile and a half long and no more than one hundred feet wide. Facing the sea, the men, women, and children were screaming to be rescued.

There were, according to reports written afterward, twenty-one war ships: two British battleships, three cruisers, and six destroyers; three French cruisers and two destroyers; an Italian cruiser and destroyer; and three American destroyers. This was in addition to smaller vessels from other countries, all massed in the harbor. Very few of them were taking on any of the desperate people on the quay.

Everywhere I looked, Turkish soldiers were shooting into the crowd or hacking at them with their swords, cutting off limbs so people would not be able to swim away. Mostly, they were snatching jewelry off the necks of the beautiful women and girls of Smyrna or grabbing the most beautiful girls and carrying them off. Ironically, the soldiers were also killing Turkish civilians who had come down to the quay, hoping to get some of the spoils of war for themselves. The Turkish soldiers thought they were Armenians even though the civilians protested, to no avail, that they were not.

I knew the French Consulate was a block away from the water, and pulling the girls with me, we went to the building. It was mobbed with people desperately trying to reach the entrance. Tossed this way and that, we managed to walk up to a young man in a French uniform. He happened to be a Kerametsi. I felt heartened, but when I asked him if the three of us could seek asylum in the consulate, the answer came back a resounding, 'No!'

Looking around at the desperate people and more importantly at the Turkish soldiers armed to the teeth with weapons, I prayed: 'Dear God, you didn't bring me all this way to abandon me!' I felt a surge of energy and I was more than determined that we weren't going to be led away and killed as so many others were. I rushed to the water's edge with the girls. The water was full of bloated and mutilated bodies, all showing signs of horrible wounds. There were suitcases and all manner of personal belongings floating around in the water. All around me was the screaming mass of humanity: some losing their minds; others jumping into the water to try to swim to one of the many ships near the harbor; and still others determined to commit suicide.

Just then, I spotted an Italian motorboat moving closer to the quay. I told the girls to jump into the water with me. They did. We started yelling as loud as we could. The Italian sailors saw us flaying our arms about and screaming. We were picked up along with a few other desperate people lucky enough to be close by. Two Italian sailors on the boat were checking to see how many ships would be needed for rescue operations.

Then the motorboat picked up speed, and as it did, I looked back at the city. The warehouses and businesses and once beautiful homes were burning. Orange and red flames mingling with black oily smoke filled the sky. The two little girls next to me were shivering from the soaking in the water as well as from the sight of the massive destruction of a great city, now receding in the distance. I was asked much later which experience had been worse for me: the massacres and deportations into the wasteland of Syria or the burning and destruction of the population and city of Smyrna. Without hesitation, I would have to say Smyrna. I don't think anyone can imagine the heartrending scenes that I witnessed. May God bless all of the victims who lost limbs, their lives, and worst of all their minds. My cousin Krikor survived the burning of Smyrna as I did. Later, while living with relatives in France, he lost his mind and died in an asylum.

Crewmen helped us climb aboard an Italian destroyer and immediately wrapped up the little girls in blankets and rushed to get us some food. A very few able-bodied men who had been rescued were on board the ship. There were hardly any pretty girls or young matrons. Most women appeared to be over forty-five years of age and were surrounded by many, many young children. I could hear Armenian and Greek spoken all around me.

As we approached the Greek port of Piraeus, I could see crowds of people gathered at the docks, waiting for ships carrying the victims from Smyrna. When we disembarked, I told the girls to hold tightly onto each other while I went off to get us something to eat. I managed to find a street vendor who took pity on me and gave me food. When I returned to the spot where I had left the little sisters, they were gone. With so many people milling about they were nowhere to be seen. To this day I hope that they were taken by good people and not harmed as so many girls were in those terrible days.

I could feel the grumbling in my stomach and looked at my miserable clothes and knew that I needed to survive. I couldn't make it here. There were so many other people in the same predicament as myself—homeless, no family, no food. I had to leave Piraeus. Maybe I could connect with my cousins later. But first I went to Salonika and stayed in Greece for about two months, working odd jobs.

I left Greece and surreptitiously went back into Turkey to Tekirdag. Some of my relatives who had left Keramet were there: Armenouhi and her husband Haji Muger, her sister Vartouhi and husband and child. Merger and Turvanda had already migrated to Kosani, Greece, where on October 7, 1922, their son Veresh was born.

Those of us who remained in Turkey stayed in one of the beautiful Armenian churches there. Then I left to go to Edirne, which was close to both Greece and Bulgaria. My cousins and their wives and husbands came there also. We stayed in another beautiful Armenian Church.

This time we remained for a short while. We knew it was going to be impossible to live in Turkey. It was time to leave. Our farewells were emotional, but we were thankful to be alive. I learned much later that the beautiful Armenian churches at Tekirdag and Edirne were destroyed by fire, by the Turks, in order to erase all evidence of Armenians ever being there. This was state policy. Since we already had a cousin in France, Merger and Turvanda and my other cousins and families would migrate there to spend the rest of their lives. I decided to go instead to Bulgaria by train."

CHAPTER 9

BULGARIA WITH
ITS PROMISE OF
A NEW LIFE

*Bulgaria, 1924. Sarkis on left, Garabed Haji Nigogos
Papazian in center, Haroutiun Taghtajian on right.
Haroutiun bought the machine gun from the Greek
soldiers in Bursa.*

"THERE ARE THREE MAIN PORT CITIES IN BULGARIA. After the whole scale destruction of Armenian communities in Turkey, Armenians gravitated to all three, and to the capital Sophia, that is also near a waterway. Varna and Bourgas are Black Sea ports and Ruse is on the Danube River. Armenians also went to Plovdiv on the Maritsa River. By 1926 the size of the Armenian community swelled to 36,000, mostly concentrated in those cities and also Haskovo and Shuman.

From the Mustapha Pasha border, which was near Edirne, I took a train to Plevna in Bulgaria and then on to Shumla. From Shumla, I went to Sophia, and then I decided to use my Nansen passport and visit my first cousin Philipos in France. His father was Ovannes, my father's brother. In France, he had changed his name to Philip Taleur. He had been a student at Robert College in Constantinople, and a couple of years before the catastrophe of 1915, he left to go to France. My plan was to stay and perhaps earn a living there.

I learned from my cousin that the owners of a mine in the countryside some distance from Paris were looking for men to work in the mine. I went there and was hired immediately. On my first day of the job, there was a tremendous avalanche in the mine. Seven workers died. Dirt and rocks came down like a flood and killed the men who were working alongside of me. I quit my job at once. The next day, I boarded an express train and returned to Sophia. I needed a job, and quickly, as I was very short on cash. Luckily for me a coffee shop needed someone to make coffee. I was hired. Most of our customers were Greek. However, one of the regular patrons was a cute, lively Bulgarian girl by the name of Panky. She became my girlfriend.

I saw my favorite film of all time in Bulgaria. It was *Les Miserables* and was in French with subtitles. That film stayed with me my whole life, and you'll learn why when you find out about my later experiences.

Unbelievable as this seems, one day, as I was reading the Armenian language newspaper, I saw an ad written by my friend, Dikran Nahabedian, looking for me. We had a joyful reunion. We lost track of one other in the hellish conflagration of Smyrna. He had been picked up by another ship and also taken to Piraeus.

We decided to room together and after a time left and went to Bourgas. We found other Kerametsis there, including Garabed Nigogos Papazian, who owned a café. I had my picture taken with Garabed and Haroutiun Taghtajian in 1924 in Bourgas. This was the same Haroutiun who had purchased the machine gun from the Greek soldiers in Bursa. Zabel Philippian, another Kerametsi, was there and married with two sons who eventually became doctors.

There was a very rich Armenian with the last name of Ajemian in Bourgas. He managed a produce market that belonged to the beautiful Armenian Church. He said that if I had been one year older, he would have made me the manager of the market.

Since Bourgas was on the Black Sea, I decided to become a fisherman. My friend Dikran and another Armenian, Antranik Minassian, from Jerakh, Turkey (near Lake Iznik), joined me on this adventure. We would take two rowboats out on the sea and fish at night. One of the boats had sails and the other did not. We caught the fish using nets. In those days, the Black Sea was teeming with fish, including these varieties: Balamud, Uskumru, and Torit. When we brought our catch to shore, vendors would buy the fish from us. To make extra money, we even transported hashish. We were always on the move.

Dikran and I went to Roosjuk (now Ruse), Bulgaria, where I located my childhood friend, Yezekel Ashirian. It was in Roosjuk, also, that I had the enormous privilege of visiting with our great Archbishop Stephannos Hark Hovagimian. He had been the prelate of Izmit, in the province of Bursa. I visited the bishop nearly every day. He became like a father to me. I could be open with him, expressing my longings and dreams for a better life.

I knew of his heroism from the times of the massacres and deportations. In Mekece, he had taken off all of his medals and placed them on the floor of the cattle car. When the Turkish officers saw the medals, many of them given to him by the Turkish sultan, he was granted an exemption from deportation, but he refused. He said that he would not abandon his flock. When they were let out of the cattle cars, he led the deportation caravan toward Bozanti. Then, he gave up his cart to those who were sick and traveled on foot to Aleppo.

From Aleppo, he was taken to Jerusalem. In 1918, when the First World War ended, he wrote a letter to Izmit, informing his parishioners that he would be returning. When he came back, hundreds of people were waiting for him, Armenians who had survived the massacres and deportations, Greeks, Turks, Jews, men, women, and children. They unhitched the horses from his carriage and pulled it to the headquarters of the Armenian Church. He was much loved.

Here are some examples of his good works. When he went to a Turkish village and saw that the villagers did not have enough water or even a mosque, he would write the government in Constantinople and let the authorities know about the destitute conditions. When inspectors came, he would indicate where water could be brought down from the mountain and even showed them where to build the mosque.

He left Turkey and went to Bulgaria when the Turkish Republic was created, accompanied by many Armenians who were fleeing also. Bulgarians in the cities complained about the ragtag groups of Armenians and told them to go to the villages. Archbishop Stepannos, who was in Varna at this time, went to the governor to complain about the treatment of the Armenians. He took the medal from around his neck that had been presented to him by the Bulgarian King Ferdinand and said: 'I don't need this anymore. Give it back to King Ferdinand.' During the Balkan War, when three hundred Bulgarian prisoners of war in Turkey could not get back home because they had no money, the archbishop hired a ship's captain. He told him to take the prisoners on board his ship back to Bourgas or Varna.

He then addressed the governor by saying: 'We were thrown out of Turkey, and now that we're in Bulgaria, you want to throw us out of the cities and force us into the villages.' When his words got back to King Ferdinand, the king said, 'Don't touch the Armenians. They have the same rights as the Bulgarians!'

I stayed in Bulgaria until I realized that I could no longer make a living there. I loved the country and the people. Oftentimes villagers would gather in one town square or another and in unison sing a folk song. It didn't take much for these good-hearted, joyful people to gather together in celebration. But the country politically was riddled with division. Aleksandr Stamboliski, the prime minister, was assassinated the first year I was there (1923). He tried to bring much change to the country. One of his measures was to give land to the peasants. Stamboliski died on the night of June 8, 1923, as a result of a coup d'etat. Aleksandr Tsankov took office. Assassinations followed, one after the other, which were dreadful events. The world economic crisis also affected Bulgaria so that many people were without work and struggling. I had to look elsewhere to survive. It was 1928. I still had my Nansen passport, which allowed me as a landless refugee to travel anywhere in the world.

In the Bulgarian newspapers in 1927, we read that an oil field of unprecedented size had been discovered near Kirkuk, Iraq. In 1928, the Iraq Petroleum Company was formed. Men were needed to work. I decided to go there. Dikran and Antranik went to France. I never saw them again.

In Bourgas, I met an Armenian who was going to Egypt, where he was delivering dozens of cases of chickens by truck. When we got to Egypt, we traveled to Port Said, where I saw graceful Egyptian women with rings in their noses. From Port Said we went to Beirut, where he dropped me off. I found a job at the Hotel Touregian, where I worked for a couple of months as a janitor. I earned my room and board but did not get paid. In Beirut I met a couple of Armenian brothers who were driving to Persia (Iran) and would travel through Iraq to get there. I hitched a ride.

I was alone again but felt optimistic because of the prospective job opportunities in Iraq. Another plus was that I knew Arabic, having been in Iraq in the aftermath of the massacres and deportations. The brothers stopped periodically to buy food, but mostly we traveled constantly, as the brothers were looking for business opportunities in Persia and didn't want to waste any time."

Among the Armenians who survived the massacres and deportations in 1915–1917, scores went to Bulgaria. After the burning of the city of Smyrna in September of 1922 by Kemalist Turkish troops, even more Armenian refugees fled to Bulgaria. Smyrna was a city heavily populated by Greeks with a lesser, but still substantial, number of Armenians before its destruction.

CHAPTER 10

IMPRISONMENT
AND SURVIVAL
IN IRAQ

Camp Vadi, Syria, 1930. Work site near the border of Iraq. Sarkis is in the center wearing a dark shirt.

"WHEN WE REACHED BAGHDAD, I THANKED THE BROTHERS AND GOT OUT OF THE CAR. Then I crossed the Tigris on a pontoon bridge that straddled the river. In the river were circular boats called *gaffa* that were manned by dark-skinned Arabs. I walked past Bedouins who were wearing robes with intricate patterns astride their Arabian horses. I entered the city through a narrow street filled with people, and flanking the street were the old walls of buildings with elaborately carved balconies. I walked further into the bazaars and saw copper and brass pots stacked one on top of the other, huge pottery jars, Persian carpets, and rows and rows of exotic fruit. Arab women, wearing veils and dark outer garments, were bartering with the vendors. I looked down at their sandaled feet and saw their *izzars* (clothes) in the beautiful colors of pink, jade, cream, and white bordered with silk and gold threads in contrast to their nondescript outer clothing.

I stopped by the kiosks of the silversmiths and admired the complex designs on their goods. Scribes at another place were writing letters on little tablets for the people who needed the service. I recognized the Arabic letters from my days as a slave in Mosul. At sunset I could hear, from a distant minaret, the call to prayer. After wandering around the narrow, balcony-lined pathways, tired and hungry, I saw in the distance what could only be described as an apparition. This specter was my brother whom I had not seen in ten years. A miracle!

'Haroutiun!' I called out. I saw that he was visibly shaken, and then he whooped and yelled out my name: 'Sarkis!' We hugged one another for the longest time as tears ran down our faces.

Haroutiun was now married and had an infant daughter, Nazin. His family lived in Mosul. His wife, Yegsabet Tokajian, was from Erzerum, Turkey. During the massacres and deportations, Yegsabet had been kidnapped by Arabs who had tortured her by poking her eyes with a thimble that had been placed in boiling water to draw out her Christian blood. She had also been subjected to sexual abuse. When the First World War ended she was placed in an orphanage in Lebanon, and it was there that she was reunited with her mother after her mother saw the scar that Yegsapet had on her thumb.

While I stayed with Haroutiun and Yegsabet I learned that there was plenty of work in the north of the country near Mosul. I had already learned to drive in Bulgaria, so it didn't take me long to get my driver's license.

The Iraqi Petroleum Company was hiring people in a place called Baiji, not far from Mosul. Calouste Gulbenkian, famously known as Mr. Five Percent, was the brain behind the company. In 1912, when he created the company, it was known as Turkish Petroleum. In the 1930s, when I was in Iraq, Mr. Gulbenkian insisted that 20 percent of the workforce in the petroleum company be of Armenian ancestry.

When I arrived in Baiji, I had to take a test before being hired. The English supervisor told me to take a tire off the truck and put it back on. I told him to do it himself. He thought that was pretty funny, and after I showed him what I could do, I was hired. Early on in my driving experience, I encountered my first dust storm. I was to pick up an English official of the petroleum company and drive him to a specific location. On the way, we were caught in a severe *sharqi* (a dry, dusty wind) that quickly changed into a violent dust storm. The gusts must have exceeded eighty kilometers an hour. The Englishman was extremely drunk and grew very frightened and irrational. I tried to do my best to calm him down and told him to take out his pocket handkerchief and wrap it around his mouth while I pulled off the road, stopped the engine, and set my emergency brake.

After spending some time whimpering and crying that he didn't want to die, he finally settled down. How ironic, I thought, after saving his life, that all I could think of was the English we encountered in Mosul, when we were starving, and how they told us that they had not come to Iraq to feed animals.

My job as a trucker consisted of carrying pipe on the truck bed. When I got to a jobsite I would undo the chain in the back and pipes would drop out. I traveled sometimes two hundred miles a day, even going into Syria and Palestine. I worked three years and earned ten dinars a month. Then, after three years, I quit. I bought myself a truck with the money I saved. It was an International truck, model C-30.

The year was 1933 and the month was August. Iraqi King Faisal was out of the country. The minister of the interior, Hikmat Sulayman, had adopted a policy aimed at the elimination of the Assyrians. The Kurd, General Bakr Sidqi, was Sulayman's point man. After engaging in several clashes with the Assyrians, he encouraged his men to kill Assyrian men, women, and children. Over three thousand were butchered in the Assyrian village of Simele (Samayyil).

In Simele, scores of Assyrians piled onto my truck bed in an effort to escape the violence. They referred to what they had gone through as a horrible massacre. I replied that I did not want to diminish their tragedy, but that the Turks had done much, much worse to the Armenians, literally destroying the very fabric of our society. I took them to Asijuh, Syria, where they got off. I wished them luck and said good-bye. A month later, in September 1933, King Faisal died while undergoing medical treatment in Switzerland. Faisal's son, Ghazi, succeeded his father as leader of Iraq. He reigned from 1933 to 1939.

Besides taking goods and passengers around the country of Iraq, I did some exploring along the way. In the Muslim holy city of Samarra, I met a Persian man my age. He told me that there would be a procession of Muslims that day that adhered to the Alevi branch of the religion. I disguised myself as a Kurd. That wasn't too difficult, as Kurds wear pants rather than the long shifts of the Arabs. I accompanied the Persian into the mosque, and when we went outside there was a large procession of the faithful carrying on with the ritual of self-flagellation. Their bodies showed signs of their heightened states of passion and were drenched with blood.

Sometime later, I was driving on a narrow road to Altun Kupri (Gold Bridge) near Kirkuk. Another truck driver was trying to pass me. Finally, I got tired of his machinations and turned my truck sharply to the left, and he turned his truck hard right to avoid hitting me. My truck was empty and his truck was filled with goods. His truck turned over and the impact killed him. I found out from eyewitnesses that the other driver was an Assyrian and was thirty-five years old. To this day, I regret my rage on the road and retain my sorrow that I had killed an innocent young man in the prime of life. If there is a hell, I will probably go there for that act alone.

I hurt my hand at the time of the accident, so I was in the hospital for a couple of days in Kirkuk. Meanwhile, my truck was confiscated. When I recovered, the Assyrian investigator sent over a guard, bearing a rifle, and he took me to court. I was found guilty by the judge of vehicular manslaughter, and I was given a prison sentence of two years. I turned over my money to my brother for safekeeping until my term of imprisonment was over. Two armed guards put me on a train in Kirkuk. I was with other prisoners and we were taken to Baghdad.

When we arrived in Baghdad, we were taken immediately to the prison. I learned that the assistant warden was Abdel Kadur, an Arab, who was about thirty-five years of age. There were one thousand other men imprisoned inside: Kurds, Assyrians, and Arabs. Besides me, a few other Armenians were there. One was named Kurken.

Our diet was the same day after day. My favorite was the *vospov* (lentil) soup. The prison garb was a long shift. The prisoners with money could buy shoes. I had given all my money to my brother in Kirkuk before I went to prison, so I was without shoes.

The ultimate punishment for a prisoner was execution. All of the prisoners would have to watch as the condemned man was brought out, hands and feet tied with ropes. He was then forced to stand on a platform. At a given signal, the bottom of the platform would open and the prisoner would drop. If his neck was not yet broken and he suffered, someone would jump on his shoulders. It's not something that you ever forget.

There was a camp of two thousand refugees in the city of Baghdad. One day, a fight broke out among the Armenians in the camp. The police brought those who started the altercation to the prison where I was incarcerated. They were to be in the prison for a couple of days, and in the room where I was kept. This room was very large with well over one hundred prisoners. I found blankets for the Armenians. When they were let out and went back to the camp, they told the other refugees about me.

There was a woman from my village of Keramet in the camp. She would visit me in prison and once brought me a pair of shoes. Whenever the refugees in the camp were able to get some good food, she would bring me some. She told me one day that she had a husband in Bulgaria and asked me to please write him a letter and tell him that she was alive. When I wrote the letter, I interjected that I thought they should get back together. In his reply, he wrote that it was too late for them to be a couple again.

One day the other prisoners and I were taken by bus and truck to the desert to work on a dam project on the Euphrates. We would work in the desert for six months. There was a big tent set up for us to sleep inside. During the day, we carried sacks of sand on our backs to build a high wall. We ate *hurma* (dates) and bread the entire time we were there.

Abdel Said was the chief of the prisoners in the desert. Many of us came down with dysentery. When I would squat down to relieve myself, nothing came out but blood. Every day, three or four men would die from this sickness. We all complained to Abdel Said. I was the most vociferous. Finally enraged at my outbursts, he grabbed hold of his long, flexible stick and proceeded to give me a terrible beating. All of his frustration was let out on me. When he was satisfied that he had taught me a lesson, he stopped. Then he brought me bread and dates. I took the food in my hands and threw it, narrowly missing his face. Then I shouted in Arabic, 'I don't need this! God can keep it!' All of the other prisoners were appalled at my words. Later, when I was back at work, Abdel Said came to apologize for the beating. I told him to forget about it.

Then, it was the day of my release. I had served nineteen months and nineteen days of my two-year sentence. An Arab got out the same time as I did. He had on only a short shift covering his body. I felt sorry for him, so I gave him my jacket, as I was wearing pants and a shirt, the clothes I had when I entered the prison. Abdul Wahab (Wahbi Effendi), the warden of the prison, saw my gesture and came over to me and asked: 'Do you know this man?' I replied that I did not. 'Then, why did you give him your jacket?'

'Because the poor guy doesn't have anything,' I replied. Abdel Wahab then motioned for his bookkeeper. 'Bring me one ticket for the train to Kirkuk for this man.' The warden gave me the train coupon and then he pressed a dinar worth five pounds into my hand (a dinar was also equivalent to five American dollars).

Before I caught the train, I went to the refugee camp in Baghdad. The leader of the Armenians wanted to take up a collection for me. But, I refused. He had been one of the men who had stayed in my room in the prison. It was an emotional farewell for all of my Armenian friends. It seemed to me that they were in a kind of prison in that refugee camp.

When I got off the train in Kirkuk, I stepped into a café for some food. It was there that I ran into an acquaintance of mine, Hovhannes, whom I had known before going to prison. Hovhannes told me that my brother had relocated to Kirkuk from Mosul. Before he left the café, Hovhannes gave me ten silver dinars to help me get back on my feet.

I found my brother's house and knocked on the door. His wife was very surprised to see me, and I thought that was strange. Then I saw my brother. He looked shocked, too. From their reaction, I realized that they probably thought I was going to die while incarcerated. But, more importantly, it was the money. After they pulled themselves together and had me sit down for a bite to eat, I asked Artin for the money that he was going to keep for me while I was away. He told me straight out that it was gone.

'What are you saying?'

'You heard me, my brother. It's gone!'

'What? Did somebody steal it?'

'No, we spent it!'

'Oh no! For Christ's sake, please don't tell me this!'

'It's true. I'm sorry!'

'Sorry! That was all the money I had in the world.'

I knew that I had to get out of there before I killed somebody or broke down in tears. So, I got up and headed for the front door.

'Wait! Where are you going?' asked my brother.

'I need a job. I'm totally broke. I'm going to Erbil. The Iraqi government is building a road there.' What I told him was true. The road would go to Rawanduz, Balakyun, Batas, Havdeyan, Geendeyan, Mavieeyan, and Mergesor.

I left them both standing there. I shut the door as I left. When I got to Erbil, there was work everywhere. I could have gotten a job easily, but I needed to buy a truck and I didn't have enough cash.

The chief of the engineers working on the highway was a Kurd by the name of Kadur Ashekhan, a man highly respected by the Kurds. He, along with his mother, Kadur Kalehan Ashekhan, was from Suleymania. He notified people that he needed twenty truckers. I became one of Kadur's personal drivers. When Kadur died some years later in Baghdad, his body was brought back to Suleymania for burial. Kurdish men, women, and children expressed their profound grief by their loud cries, wailing and throwing dirt on their faces and heads. In Arabic this demonstrative form of grief is known as *maltamah*.

This is the story of how I was able to buy a truck. I went to the four engineers who worked for Kadur. They were fairly well off and had a great deal of merchandise in their office. So I asked each man for a loan of twenty dinars so that I could buy a truck. I told them that I would pay back the loan with interest. They all gave me the money. Then I went to Baghdad and looked up a family man I knew by the name of Konyala Hagop. I told him to go to the Ford Motor Company and tell them the following: 'I have a customer who wants to buy a Ford pick-up truck. If I bring him here, how much money will you give me?' If the manager replies, 'How much do you want?' I told Hagop to ask for five dinars and not to accept if the manager offered anything less. The Ford management gave Hagop the five dinars, and with the money I was able to buy the truck.

When I took on a passenger, I asked for a dinar for the fare. So besides making a salary delivering supplies for the highway, which when completed would go from Erbil to Kurdistan, I made extra money transporting people. On my truck I carried forty-foot long, twelve-inch wide steel rods that were needed for bridges over high precipices, such as the Ruwanduz gorge. I became familiar with the geography of the country driving that truck. In the west and southwest of Iraq is the desert. Between the upper Tigris and Euphrates is the rolling upland. In the north and northeast of the country are the highlands, where I did most of my driving. However,

I did go into the central and southeastern alluvial plain areas through which the Tigris and Euphrates flow.

After the death of Kadur, someone told me, 'Every Goddamn policeman salutes you when you drive around. Watch out, Sarkis. No more Kadur Effendi!' I looked this man straight in the face and told him, 'Kadur's dead alright, but his God is looking after me.'

One hundred percent I believe that the Kurds have a right to their lands in Iraq. My brother-in-law, Edward Shamlian, remembered seeing a group of Kurds with their hands bound by ropes being taken out of Zakho, Iraq, by Arabs late in the 1930s. Who knows what happened to them? The Kurds suffered greatly. However, they behaved horribly. In our historic homelands of eastern Turkey, the Armenians and Kurds were the majority population, not the Turks. This was before the genocide. The Kurds did not have to turn against us in the brutal way they did. Basically, they became murderous henchmen for the despotic Young Turk government, and well before that during the Hamidian massacres also. Sadly, they paid a very high price when Ataturk hung all of the Kurdish leaders in the 1920s followed by even worse treatment by Ataturk in Dersim (now called Tunceli Province in eastern Turkey) in 1937–1938, when over thirteen thousand Kurds and hidden Armenians were massacred.

From 1935 until my wife, children, and I came to America in 1941, I spent a considerable amount of time in Mosul. This city is 250 miles northwest of Baghdad and stands on the west bank of the Tigris River, opposite the ancient city of Nineveh on the east bank. The Tigris River, at this point, is a wide and powerful river. Mosul was the historic center for the Nestorian Christianity of the Assyrians, and according to tradition contains the tombs of Jonah (at Nebi Younis) and Nahum. Nebi Younis was the place where we Armenians congregated upon our arrival following the deportations.

Long before the Muslim conquest of the seventh century, the Assyrians of the old city of Nineveh had converted to Christianity during the first and second centuries. Saint George's Monastery (Mar Gurguis) is one of the oldest churches in Mosul and is located to the north of the city.

Armenians first came to Mosul in 1604, when Shah Abbas forced their relocation from their historic homeland to Persia (Iran). From there some Armenians subsequently moved further south to settle in Mesopotamia (Iraq). After the massacres and forced deportations of the Armenians of the period 1915 to 1923, more than twenty-five thousand additional Armenians came to Iraq. Mosul remained under Ottoman control until 1918 and was the capital of a *vilayet* or province of the same name (one of the three provinces of Ottoman, Iraq). By the end of the First World War, British forces occupied Mosul. After the war, the city and the surrounding areas became part of the British mandate of Iraq.

Something that should be of interest to linguists is that the Arabic of Mosul carries the influence of the languages of all the various ethnic groups that have lived in the city: Kurds, Turkmens, Armenians, Chaldeans, and others. For example, under the influence of the Armenian language, Mosul Arabic often replaces "r" with "gh."

When I was there, in the 1930s, Mosul was not only a city on the Tigris River, but it was also the name of a state in Iraq. There were three hundred thousand people in the state of Mosul. Sheikhs controlled many of the states in Iraq. One sheikh might control a hundred thousand people. Sheikh Hadji was the person in charge of the Arabs in Mosul. He was over six feet tall. We Armenians lived in the Christian section of the city with two Armenian Apostolic churches. There were a couple of hundred of us there, but there were twenty-five thousand Armenians in the state of Mosul.

I would transport people and goods in my truck from one place to another. Once I had 113 people on my truck. Most of my passengers were Arabs who were working on the road from Mosul to Kurdistan. Another time I picked up a young Arab girl running away from an abusive older husband.

I often went into Iran to the cities of Rumia and Tabriz. One day I even took the British consul's assistant to Tabriz, a city much like San Francisco, with many hills. I also spent a lot of time driving from Erbil to Ruwanduz. For that trip, I charged a half dinar for the ride. The supervisors of the Arab workers would collect the fare money from their workers and pay me.

My brother, Haroutiun, his wife, and young family moved to Mosul. He was in bad shape for a man with a family. At that time he didn't have a passport or any money. I gave him ten dinars and told him: 'I'm swallowing a pound of sand every day, working for this money. I want it back. Get a job!' He did get a job on the pipeline driving a truck. But every penny he earned, he spent on liquor. One time, some Arabs rushed to where I was and said that my brother was in danger of being killed. In a drunken state, he was insulting Mohammed and the religion of Islam. I rushed over to the café, got him out of there, and took him home.

Mosul had a very diverse population when I was there. Besides the Armenians, there were the Yazidis, a group of people heavily discriminated against but very accepting of other beliefs. They kept my cousin Faron from harm during the genocide until 1918. As a matter of fact, the Yazidis would adamantly refuse to give up to the Turks any of the Armenian children that they had taken in during those horrendous times.

The Yazidis believe in a supreme being who from his own essence produced seven gods or angels of which the principal one was called Melak Taus. Something that was quite stunning to me was their practice of the 'rain charm.' During a dry season, a boy and girl would go from house to house in their village and would perform a dance at the end of which each householder would throw water on them. This was so like the traditional 'Churpoteek' of our village of Keramet when I was a child. Yazidi washing practices were similar to ours also. Yazidi women would use wooden clubs as they beat their family washing at the springs. And the soap they used were great tablets of homemade olive-oil soap. They would spread the washed garments on the hot rocks to dry.

Another group in the Mosul region were the Jews. Most of the towns in South Kurdistan had significant Jewish populations. They were petty merchants and peddlers, and in the larger towns one would see their synagogues. There were English archeologists working in and around Mosul during the 1930s. Once, when I crossed the bridge to get from Mosul to the ancient site of Nineveh, I conversed in Arabic with an English archeologist. He told me of an ancient scale that he had just discovered on that site.

On one of my routes, I drove into the village of Tell Keif, a large village that was comprised of Chaldean Christians, with a population of seven thousand people. This was where my brother Nazar died in 1916. What a treat to go into the village and see all of the girls in ankle-length dresses of bright colors: yellows, greens, and reds adorned with silver girdles. Gold necklaces and jeweled rings worn through their right nostrils completed their costume."

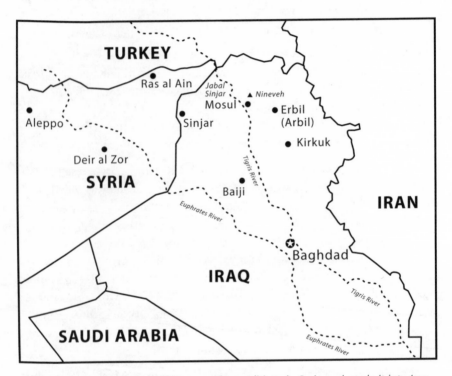

Some Armenians who survived the terrible conditions in Syria and made it into Iraq gravitated toward the Jabal Sinjar region, where they were taken in by the Yazidi. Or they went to Mosul, where Christian Assyrians and Christian and Muslim Arabs gave them food and water.

CHAPTER 11

ERBIL AND
THE HOTEL FARAH

Erbil, alternately spelled Arbil or Irbil, is one of the most ancient cities of the world.

"ON THE ROAD FROM MOSUL, I OFTEN TRAVELED TO ERBIL, which is 211 miles north of Baghdad and fifty miles east of Mosul. It is one of the oldest continuously inhabited cities in the world, with a history dating back to 5000 BCE. Erbil was second only to the Assyrian city of Ashur as a great religious center. *Arba'ilu* in Assyrian means four gods, and in its glory days the goddess Ishtar reigned supreme.

Kermanji is the language in general use throughout South Kurdistan. In the districts of Erbil, Altun Kupri, Kirkuk, and Kifri, the Turkoman dialect is spoken along with Kurdish. In Kirkuk, Arabic, Kurdish, Turkish, and Persian are spoken.

On an eventful day for me, sometime in 1936, I stopped off in Erbil with a truck filled with goods. I was hungry and looking for a café for a bite to eat. Erbil at that time was made up of Kurds, Muslim Arabs, Christian Arabs, and a sprinkling of Armenians. The café I stopped at was in the heart of the city. Erbil was formed from an ancient tell or occupied mound rising anywhere from eighty-two to one hundred feet above the surrounding plain. Erbil is also noted for its citadel and its stone walls that circumscribe the occupied mound on which the city stands. A spectacular vista unfolds on all sides, as Erbil sits at the foothills of the mountains in the east. I could see Jebel Makhoul on the other side of the Tigris. Everyone in the region was well aware of the fact that near their city was the site where the Macedonian king, Alexander the Great, fought the Battle of Gaugamela and defeated the Persian King, Darius III. This victory led to Alexander's conquest of Persia. This battle was fought on the plain between Mosul and Erbil in 331 BCE.

While I was sitting in the café and having finished a delicious bowl of soup, I leaned forward to light my cigarette when all at once two hands grabbed me by the neck. Startled, I turned around. I saw at once that it was Hovhannes Haroutiun Kapikian, the man who had pressed the dinars into my hands in Kirkuk to help tide me over after my release from prison. I motioned for him to join me at the table. He was as personable as ever. He sat down and took out a cigarette that I quickly lit it for him.

Like me, Haroutiun had been born in Turkey, in the city of Izmit, to be exact. He had lost most family members during the massacres and deportations.

But now in Iraq, he saw that there were many opportunities to make money even if one was a Christian Armenian. He motioned to the proprietor, who was a Kurd, and asked him in Kurdish to bring us two cups of coffee.

'Sarkis, you're looking much better than the last time I saw you when you were just skin and bone.'

'Thanks, Haroutiun.'

'I understand that your trucking business is doing well. Good for you, my boy! But, I have another proposition for you to consider.'

'What is it?'

'Hagop, the Kharpetsi, who manages the Hotel Farah here in Erbil, is very sick with tuberculosis.'

'I'm sorry about that. You do mean Hagop who has two step sons, Ramsi and Wahab, and another son, George, with his Arab Christian wife?'

'That's him. The owner of the hotel is very concerned about Hagop's health and is looking around for someone to take his place. How'd you like to co-manage the hotel with me? I think it could be a real moneymaker.'

It didn't take me but a minute to think about his proposal. 'Haroutiun, I like you. You are a very helpful and generous man and honest too. I can work with you. I'll curtail my trucking business until I see how much work is involved in running the hotel.' I could see that Haroutiun was pleased with what I said. 'Deal then?' he asked.

'Deal!' We shook hands on it.

Soon after we learned of the death of Hagop, the Kharpetsi. His luck had run out. Now Haroutiun and I went to the owner, Shabab, the Turk, and happily, he liked us both. He let us rent a room together at the hotel for five dinars a month. The name of the hotel was Farah. That word in Arabic means comfortable, exactly what we hoped to nurture in our patrons, the feeling of being comfortable while staying with us. The building was made of gray marble and had thirty-two rooms. At first we charged half a dinar a night for a room, but on the advice on an Arab sheikh, we raised the rate to three fourths of a dinar.

Two cooks worked for us, both men. One was an Arab and the other an Armenian by the name of George Nazar, whom we called Babik. Nazar formerly managed a hotel himself, but now he gave it up and began working for us full time. He also had a home in Mosul.

We charged extra for the food, and our meals were well prepared and didn't vary. For breakfast, we served soup. Lunch consisted of rice pilaf and *lulu* or shish kebab, with dinner basically the same as lunch: rice pilaf and a variety of meat dishes. We ran a clean establishment and dealt with honest vendors who supplied us with whatever we needed. However, one time my partner, Haroutiun, ordered twenty blankets from a traveling salesman by the name of Abkar Gareebian. We never received those blankets. Abkar turned out to be a first-class crook, and believe it or not, his brother was the richest man in Iraq at that time, importing and exporting cement, lumber, and steel.

Sheets were changed daily and were washed by Arab Christian women. I even set up a makeshift shower on the roof, using a hose, so that our patrons could bathe. Meals were served in our big dining room, the floor of which was covered with squares of colored marble. There was a sheikh by the name of Suleiman who, whenever he stayed at the hotel, made a habit of spitting on the floor in the dining room. Finally, I had enough, and as inconspicuously as possible said to him: 'Sheikh, forgive me for having to tell you this, but if you keep spitting on this marble floor, someone is liable to slip on your spit and end up breaking his neck.' He apologized and said, 'Sarkis, I will never do it again.' And he didn't.

I think our guests really enjoyed staying at the hotel. Once Haroutiun told me there was a man in one of the rooms who knew me. I went looking for him, and when he came out of his room, we recognized one another immediately. We had both been in the orphanage in Mosul, in 1918. It was good to see Karam again. Another time one of our patrons was a famous newspaper reporter from Baghdad.

An important man in Erbil was a Kurd by the name of Goojuk Mullah. He was in control of many people. He had hired an Arab by the name of Shabah, who would call the faithful to prayer from the minaret. Shabah had a beautiful voice, and Goojuk Mullah appreciated a man with a good voice. However, Shabah liked his alcohol. One day he drank so much that he was unable to call the worshippers to prayer, slurring his words and sounding totally incomprehensible. Goojuk Mullah fired him on the spot. It was later the same day that Shabah came and begged me to intercede on his behalf. I went to Goojuk Mullah's home and told him that Shabah had a very bad cold and that was why he had sounded so terrible. Shabah was hired back. When I got married, on July 3, 1938, in Mosul, I gave up my partnership in the hotel. I was traveling enough already in my trucking business, and it would have been too difficult for me to commute between Erbil and Mosul, where I lived with my wife, Evelyn.

Haroutiun understood and took over the management of the hotel. I have very fond memories of this experience and all of the men and women with whom I worked. I wish I could say the same for the relations between the Christians and the Muslim Arabs. There were always altercations against Christians in Erbil.

Since I did so much traveling between Erbil and Mosul, I was always interested in learning about Armenians and other minorities in these regions and how they managed to survive in a Muslim country. Near Mosul there were two Armenian villages, Seghert and Havras. The Armenians of Seghert spoke Arabic, and the Armenians of Havras had built an Apostolic church there. I wonder now if any Armenians remain. I doubt it, as gradually many of them immigrated to Armenia.

In Mosul during those years, the Assyrians had a very forthright and strong leader. His name was Mar Shimon. His sister was a tough person who could really handle a rifle. She went by the name of Surmah Khanum. There was always jockeying for power among the Assyrians, so they never presented a united front. An Assyrian, by the name of Agha Petros, wanted to take the place of Mar Shimon. Years later, Bishop Mar Shimon was assassinated in California.

There was more than enough commerce in Iraq during that time to keep me busy in my trucking business. The English there were supervising work on the oil pipeline. And there was always a need for my services to transport people taking them from one work site to another.

As mentioned before, I traveled into Iran and saw the cities of Tabriz and Rumia. Both places had large Armenian populations. Tabriz was incredibly beautiful. There's a Persian saying that gives an idea of its loveliness:

Edger Isfahan nebeedanee

Tabris misfigihan.

Translation:

If there wasn't Isfahan

Tabris would be half the world.

I didn't keep in touch with my friends in Iraq after I immigrated to America. I know that my truck driver friend, Yegisheh, originally from Adabazar, Turkey, died in Iraq, and his children immigrated to America and opened a delicatessen in Pasadena, California. About the time I came to America, my hotel partner, Haroutiun, was married and had a daughter. I wonder if his daughter remained in Iraq or whether she immigrated to Armenia, as that's where many Armenians were going."

Bulgaria, 1930s. Archbishop of Izmit, Stephannos Hark Hovagimian. Written on back of photo: "You probably know this man. You had the good fortune of living with him for a long time. Let's see if you remember."

Bolis (Istanbul), 1923. Central Prison. Hagop Nigogossian is sewing.

New York, 1921. Aghavni and her third husband, Artin Dirtadian.

New York, date unknown. In center, Florence Pashayan, one of the daughters of Aghavni Dirtadian with her children. Left to right: Deran, Ann Lewis, Arthur, and Susan Sady.

France, 1965. Vartouhi (Armenouhi's sister) with husband Hagop Peselian, son Ara, and grandson.

Nice, France, 1965. Armenouhi Atamian (Sarkis's first cousin) standing alongside her husband, Haji Muger Atamian.

Iraq, late 1940s. The family of Haroutiun (Artin) Markarian (Sarkis's only surviving brother). Left to right, back row: Kohar, Markar, Alice. Left to right, front row: Nazin, Haroutiun's wife Yegsapet, and Haroutiun.

Paris, France, 1942.
Hagop Nigogossian.

Bourgas, Bulgaria,
November 27, 1951.
Sarkis's first cousin Garabed
S. Mesrobian. On back:
"A souvenir for my father's
brother's son Sarkis Markar
Sarkisian. May I stay alive."

Sophia, Bulgaria, 1924. Dikran Nahabedian (born in Karsak near Keramet), Sarkis seated in center, and standing on right, Antranik Minassian (born in Jerakh near Keramet village).

Camp Vadi, Syria, 1930. Jobs were plentiful with the formation of the Iraqi Petroleum Company. Sarkis is standing in the middle row wearing a dark shirt.

Mosul, Iraq, 1938. Sarkis leaning on his truck with Arab passengers.

Mosul, Iraq, 1938. Sarkis standing, Yegisheh at his feet with other truck drivers having a picnic.

Camp Vadi, Syria near border with Iraq. Tractor lifting pipes for the oil pipeline.

Mosul, Iraq, 1938. Sarkis standing some distance from his truck with unidentified men.

Mosul, Iraq, 1938. Sarkis sitting next to Yegisheh at the picnic.

Mosul, Iraq, 1938. A Kurdish man on the left and Sarkis on a donkey while Yegisheh stands alongside.

Mosul, Iraq, 1937.
Evelyn Shamlian's engagement photo.

Mosul, Iraq, 1939. Minas Papazian, Ellen
Shakeh and Arthur Minas's godfather.

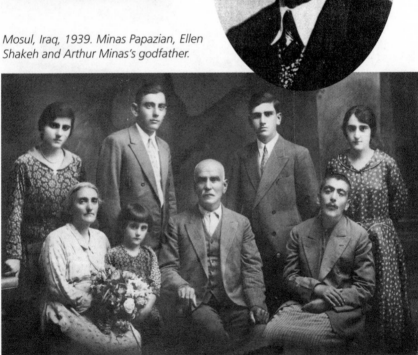

Aleppo, Syria, 1928. Evelyn's family. Back row, left to right: Rebecca, Toros, Edward,
Evelyn. Front row, left to right: Hiranoush, her youngest daughter Arlene, her
husband Hagop, and Hrant (the epileptic son).

Mosul, Iraq. Sarkis's driver's license.

Aleppo, Syria, 1930. Left to right: Evelyn Shamlian, her sister, Rebecca, and, sitting, their friend Sirvart.

Mosul, Iraq, 1938. Picnic honoring Sarkis's father, Markar. Sarkis wearing an Iraqi cap. Evelyn cooking alongside of him. Rebecca in back, with sister Arlene next to her. Sitting on ground: Edward holding a bottle next to Yegisheh, also holding a bottle.

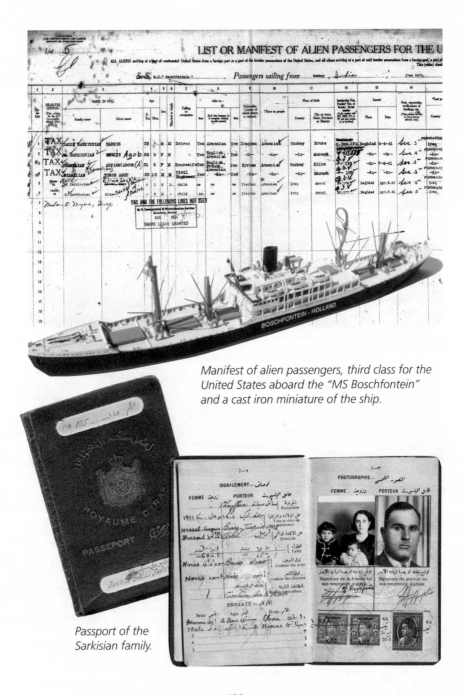

Manifest of alien passengers, third class for the United States aboard the "MS Boschfontein" and a cast iron miniature of the ship.

Passport of the Sarkisian family.

CHAPTER 12

MARRIED TO AN
EDUCATED WOMAN
FROM MARASH

*Mosul, Iraq, July 3, 1938. Wedding picture of Evelyn
and Sarkis.*

1937–1940. "I WAS MAKING SUCH GOOD MONEY in my trucking and hotel business that I started thinking seriously about settling down. But first I needed to find a nice girl from a good family.

Many Armenians didn't think that truckers would make good husbands, as we had a reputation of being tough guys: frequenting whorehouses, swearing, and generally being a rambunctious lot. There was a reason for this. The Arabs all knew very well what had happened in Turkey between 1915 and 1923: the whole scale defilement and kidnapping of our women and girls, the murderous rampages and robberies on the deportation routes benignly looked on by the Turkish gendarmes. Consequently, the Arabs thought Armenian men were weak-kneed cowards. So, we Armenian truckers did everything we could to put that notion to rest, often at great personal sacrifice.

It was only later in Iraq in conversation with a powerful Arab sheikh that I learned the true magnitude of what had befallen our Armenian people. To this day I do not know how he came to own a book with the horrendous photographs of our victims, photographs that had been taken at the time of the genocide. The photographs must have been taken surreptitiously, because it was the express policy of the Young Turk government to forbid any kind of picture taking. I have to say I learned much more than I wanted about what had happened to my people in my discussions with this sheikh.

In order to be attractive to a young woman, I had to do something about my appearance. All of my clothes were practical and made of coarse fabric. In the climate in which I worked they were just fine, but if I was going to go into polite society, I needed to upgrade my image. A very good Armenian tailor in Mosul, Dajod Andonian, had already made a black wool coat for me to wear in cold weather. So I went to his shop and told him I needed a suit. I selected brown wool, pinstriped in a cream color, of fine quality. Dajod fitted me and made a muslin pattern, from which he tailored the suit. A shirt was made in a pastel color with a matching pocket handkerchief. Dajod had a selection of ties, all imported, and I chose one that would go with the suit. When the suit was completed and I tried it on, I knew that I looked good.

There was to be a concert featuring a very popular female singer from Syria in a few weeks. A trucker's wife told me that I would be able to see young ladies from good families in attendance.

When I arrived, the auditorium was filled to capacity. I looked around and saw many women, but two really made me pause. They were nice looking and in their mid-twenties. Before the concert began, they were walking around and speaking to people they knew and, in subtle ways, showing off. I stared at them and asked an acquaintance who they were. He replied that they were the daughters of Hagop Shamlian, originally from Marash, Turkey. His was the only Christian-owned tannery out of fifty in that city. In 1915, the Shamlians avoided deportation because Hagop's leather was superior and was consequently chosen by the Turkish government for boots for Turkish soldiers. Hagop had hired many Armenian men to save them not only from conscription in the army where they would be put into labor battalions and then killed, but also from deportation, where the outcome was also death. He was an unsung hero of Marash during those terrible times.

The girls certainly did have an admirable pedigree. Especially flashy was the taller of the two young ladies: olive skinned with dark brown hair and beautiful, flashing eyes. But I noticed that she wasn't as graceful when she moved around, appearing kind of clumsy. The other sister was more delicate, with pale skin and dark brown hair. She was wearing a cream-colored blouse ruffled at the neckline and a slim, calf-length black wool skirt. The trucker's wife told me she was an accomplished seamstress and probably made her elegant outfit. She had beautiful posture and was smiling and friendly to all with whom she was conversing. But I still looked at her more beautiful sister, thinking to myself about arranging to meet her at the home of her family in Mosul.

My friend, seeing that I was interested, told me that the beautiful one, Rebecca, was also hot-tempered and willful. He suggested that I needed to look at the other one more seriously, as she was of an easygoing and sweet nature. Her name was Evelyn Shamlian and she was the eldest daughter of Hagop and his second wife, Hiranoush. Evelyn was born in Marash, in 1910. Her mother was originally from Kilis, Turkey, and the daughter of a very pious Protestant family. I told my companion to intercede on my behalf and ask her father if I could visit their home. My friend worked it out and soon a visit was arranged.

Hagop sat between Evelyn and myself and wouldn't leave us alone. She spoke beautiful Armenian and also fluent Turkish and said that after graduating from the American Girls High School in Aleppo, Syria, she taught school in Jarablus and Berejik, Syria, and did some teaching in Mosul also.

It was only when her father momentarily turned his head away from me that I looked straight at her and winked. She looked down at the beautifully patterned Kurdish tribal carpet and placed a delicate hand up to her mouth to stifle a giggle. Then, dutiful daughter that she was, she left the sitting room and went into the kitchen to prepare Turkish coffee. Returning some time later, she carried a brass tray with three tiny cups and saucers and a plate with exquisite pastries that she had prepared. I thought the visit was a success.

I would return again a week later. It was then that her father left the room and I boldly sat next to her, gently put my arms around her, and planted a kiss on her cheek. At first, she didn't fight me off and seemed rather pleased, but then pushed me away, expressing shock.

After a reasonable time had passed, I announced to her father, Hagop, that I would like to be engaged to his daughter. He told me that he would tell me her answer after he spoke to his daughter first. She agreed to my offer. We were officially engaged. After that, I lavished money on her for clothes and jewelry. She purchased lovely fabric and made herself very stylish clothes. She also knew that the best jewelers were in Aleppo, Syria, where they had gone after the massacres and deportations. So Evelyn took a train to Aleppo and purchased gold earrings and bracelets for herself.

But, as in all good things, there is always jealousy and nefarious people who want to take advantage of an opportunity for one of their own. Word got out in the Armenian community of our engagement and of my generosity. Someone with a daughter younger than Evelyn by about ten years, as Evelyn was twenty-six at this time, went to Hagop and spread unfavorable information about me. Perhaps this family thought that I would be interested in marrying a child. I was not. Hagop was not happy about what he heard about me. When he told Evelyn, she became very upset also, and the next time she saw me, she broke off our engagement, returning the jewelry that she so loved wearing.

To say I was deeply offended and angry is a gigantic understatement. I told her brothers Toros and Edward that I would break their legs if she did not take me back. Because of my reputation as a tough guy, they took the threat very, very seriously and got on their knees and begged her to change her mind. She did.

Evelyn was raised a Protestant and I was raised in the Apostolic Church. We were married in the Armenian Apostolic Church in Mosul on July 3, 1938. It was a beautiful event. She wore a white satin floor-length bridal gown created by the best seamstress in Mosul. Evelyn provided expert guidance in designing the dress. I was over the moon with happiness, marrying such a lovely, sweet, good-natured, educated, and refined woman who also was a wonderful cook and family oriented. I knew how lucky I was.

We rented a house made of *jez* (cement) with three rooms on the street called Road a Ghazi; it had an indoor toilet and a shower. On hot nights we'd sleep on the roof. Whenever I brought extra chickens home from one of my truck routes, Evelyn would have her family over for dinner. She was very generous and loved her family very much. She even gave food to my brother's family, who were always in dire need.

Evelyn and I were compatible in all ways. I could finally relax and be myself. I even told her about my experiences with other women. She listened intently and never judged me. It is possible for a person to be all things to someone. She was everything to me: my wife, my mother and father, my brothers, my friend, and my lover. However, the horrible experiences of my younger years did not leave me. Oftentimes I would wake up drenched in sweat, and Evelyn told me that night after night I would moan and yell out in my sleep. Undoubtedly I was reliving the terrors that would never go away.

Nine months after we married, on May 19, 1939, my eldest daughter Shakeh (aka Ellen) was born, and eighteen months after that, on November 9,

1940, my son Minas (aka Arthur) was born. I celebrated long and hard after the birth of my son. Evelyn wondered what had happened to me. I went out drinking with my friends and was gone the whole night of his birth. Evelyn felt abandoned by me, but she said she had never seen anything like the desperate happiness I felt.

Sadly, the midwife, using forceps, had damaged the right shoulder of my son as she pulled him from my wife's body. Minas would have this visible difference in his shoulders for the rest of his life because of this midwife's ineptitude. My children were baptized in the Armenian Church in Mosul. I asked a friend, Minas Papazian, to be my children's godfather. He gladly accepted the responsibility.

Evelyn helped me in so many ways. She encouraged my desire to acknowledge those who had helped me in the past. I searched for and found Khadeeje's home. She was the Arab woman who had cured my trachoma. Before I visited her, I went to the bazaar and bought an *abaya* (the black robe worn by Arab women). Then, I bought a container of *halvah* (a dessert-like paste made of sesame seed). Finally, I purchased a pair of women's shoes. I then hired a man to carry these gifts to the home of the *Jamus* woman, Khadeeje. After tipping the carrier, I knocked on the door. Khadeeje's husband and two grown sons answered. I told them I had gifts for Khadeeje. She came to the door, older now but still friendly faced. She had absolutely no idea who I was until I told her how she had helped me as a child. She still didn't recognize me until I pointed to my eyes. 'Oh my God!' she exclaimed, and she grabbed hold of me and kissed me. I told her I had gifts for her and took out the new *abaya*, the shoes, and the container of *halvah*. She was delighted with the gifts and happily introduced me to her husband and children.

I would also visit Ahmed Beg's home, where I had toiled as a slave with my brother, Haroutiun. I really wanted to treat them to the movies. After I introduced myself and with much gaiety on their part, I said: 'There's a very good movie in town. I would be honored if you would be my guests.' They replied: 'We don't go to those kinds of places!' I said, 'I'm going to buy the tickets. You won't have to spend one cent. Let your son, Hussein, decide.' He was the eldest of the children. He approved.

The movie was from Egypt and was in Arabic. Before the film began, I bought candy for everybody. The story of the film was very sad. The star was the great singer, Mohammed Abdel-Wahab. In the story, he was a slave. When he began singing in Arabic, the whole group with me started crying. When the movie ended, they began kissing me and telling me it was a night they would never forget.

Mosul was a vibrant place for Armenians in the 1930s. My father-in-law had a tanning business in Mosul, and his youngest son, Edward, worked for him. Toros, Edward's older brother, was an engineer; Rebecca was a single woman living at home; and the youngest daughter, Arlene, was in school. There were two siblings living in America at that time: one was their eldest half-brother, Puzant, and his sister Helen. Puzant would later sponsor us when we were ready to leave Iraq and come to America.

The Armenian Church where Evelyn and I were married was Gregorian and affiliated with the National Church in Echmiadsin, Armenia. I don't recall the Der Hayr's name, but I'm sure he had been born in Turkey.

Because the community of Armenians in Mosul was rather small, everybody knew each other's business. For example, to this day I recall the names of the children of the Tajeerian family. They had lived in Baghdad but moved to Mosul to raise their children. Here are the names: a girl was named Zununt, which means birth; a boy was named Yercanik, which means happy; a boy was named Veresh, which means revenge; a boy was named Khunteer, which means situation; a boy was named Lini, which means may it be; a boy was named Azat, which means free; and a boy was named Hairenik, which means fatherland.

Sadly, the political situation in Iraq was becoming ever more precarious for the Armenians. In August 1937, a military group murdered General Bakr Sidqi, the Kurd leader who had been the instigator of the massacre of the Assyrians that happened in 1933. Then in April of 1939, King Ghazi was killed in an automobile accident and was succeeded by his infant son, Faisal II.

Ghazi's first cousin, Amir Abdel Ilah, was made regent. Arabs poured into the city center of Mosul, brandishing their swords and screaming for

Christian blood. They thought the English were responsible for Ghazi's auto accident.

We Christians had always been treated as second-class citizens. To drive this point home I recall an incident. Shaklava was a city close to Mosul. I wanted to buy a five-acre plot of land there where I could have an apple orchard. I had a meeting with the sheikh of Shaklava, who was Miranee Gaderbek, a Kurd, and generations back of Armenian ancestry. He discouraged me from purchasing that land. He indicated that only Muslims had the right to purchase large amounts of land. That ended the discussion.

With the sword-wielding Arabs crying for Christian blood as well as the Kurdish sheikh discouraging me from buying land, I saw the handwriting on the wall. I did not want to subject my wife and young family to another round of massacres and deportations as we had gone through in Turkey in 1915 and my wife had experienced in Marash in 1920. I decided it was time to leave Iraq. My in-laws felt the same way.

Luckily for all of us, Hagop had a sister, Ferideh, who had immigrated to America after the Adana Massacres of 1909 and was living in Fresno, California. She was married to Jim Vagim, the owner of a packinghouse, and he was financially comfortable. Mr. Vagim had lost both his mother and father during the Hamidian Massacres of 1894–1896. Evelyn's half-brother Puzant lived in San Francisco, having left the Middle East in the early 1920s. So we had people in America who could sponsor us.

My brother-in-law Toros, the engineer, had since married a beautiful Armenian girl a number of years younger than himself. He doted over her. We would be traveling to America with both Toros and his wife, Arpine Adrouni."

CHAPTER 13

COMING TO
AMERICA AND
A NEW LIFE

Passport picture, Mosul, Iraq, 1941. Evelyn, née Agob,
Arthur Minas, Deli Sarkis, and Ellen Shakeh.

"IN 1941, BEFORE OUR MOMENTOUS JOURNEY BEGAN, we gave our household items to my brother's family. Evelyn insisted, however, that we take with us one hundred pounds of lambs' wool for comforters in America. Toros accompanied his wife, Arpine, Evelyn carried baby Minas, and I held onto the hand of my two-year-old daughter, Shakeh, as we climbed on board a train in Mosul that took us to Baghdad. We remained there in a hotel for fifteen days. In Baghdad, the United States consulate office issued us quota immigrant visas. They would be collected upon our arrival in America. It was good that we were leaving, because in the same year of 1941, the Arabs wanted the English out of Iraq and the political situation was precarious.

From Baghdad, we secured passage on a cargo ship that took us to Karachi, India, where we stayed in a hotel for twenty days. Luckily I started out with five hundred dinars in my pocket, as my money was going fast. From Karachi, we went to Bombay, where we remained for two months. One day, when I was out walking with my young son on my shoulders, we found out from the excited people on the street that Mahatma Gandhi would be speaking. So I followed the crowds with my little son and we were able to catch a glimpse of him. On another occasion, I rode in a carriage driven by a camel. My wife, Evelyn, laughed when she saw how at ease I was even holding onto a cup of coffee.

Finally the day arrived when we would board the Dutch freighter *MS Boschfontein*. We found out that it was built in 1928 in Rotterdam, the Netherlands. It would carry 144 passengers in two classes. Its former name was *Nieuwkerk* (1929–1934). It was rebuilt as *Boschfontein* in 1934 as a cargo ship and then was converted into a passenger ship in the same year for the Holland-Africa run.

We were on the high seas. A young Dutch steward, whose first name was Bill, looked after our young family, making sure that Evelyn and our children had fresh oranges daily. Evelyn was able to communicate with Bill, however haltingly, as English was one of the languages she learned at the American Girls High School in Aleppo.

The officers on board would flirt with my beautiful sister-in-law, Arpine, when she was sunning herself on deck. On another occasion, a sailor rushed over to me and told me that my daughter, Shakeh, was near the fantail and hanging onto the railing, perilously close to falling overboard. I rushed over to where she was and as quietly as possible, so as not to frighten her, grabbed her from off the railing.

We traveled to some beautiful ports: Ceylon, Colombo, Indonesia, Singapore, the Philippines, and Hawaii. I would have to say that Ceylon was the most beautiful. I don't know how Evelyn managed with two very young children. What a job! When we started out, Minas was four and a half months old, and when we arrived in San Francisco, he was nine months old.

On August 16, 1941, we disembarked in San Francisco and were greeted with much happiness by Evelyn's half-brother, Puzant, and Auntie Ferideh. My father-in-law, Hagop, my mother-in law, Hiranoush, and my sister-in-law Rebecca, who had arrived in America before us, were also there. We stayed in Puzant's Victorian home near the corner of Sixteenth and Market Streets. It was then that Evelyn insisted that we see a doctor for Minas' shoulder. We did, and that visit ate up the last of my money. The doctor did nothing whatsoever to fix my son's shoulder.

It's a lucky thing that I had a job lined up at Jim Vagim's packinghouse in Fresno. Ferideh took us to the train station, and I clearly remember how Minas and Shakeh started screaming when they heard the train whistle. Jim Vagim's packinghouse was huge. I would work with another man alongside a conveyer belt, where boxes would be moved. We would stack up the boxes of produce and then a truck would come and take the boxes away. I even drove a truck while I worked there, transporting produce. I made fourteen dollars a week.

Ferideh's best friend was a heavyset woman with incredibly beautiful dark eyes named Hatun Bazarian, aka Hatun Chavoush. They were both plain speaking, good women, without any artifice, and happiest attending the Armenian Protestant church or talking about their faith. What I remember with fondness are the hot Fresno nights when our families would sit on the porch and talk about the old country. Forget about the job. I hated it.

Hatun was famous in the immigrant Marash community for her exploits in the old country. She had been an absolutely fearless young woman. Carrying a rifle and dressed as a Turkish soldier, she forced her way into Turkish homes and freed Armenian children and young women who had been kidnapped. Because of her actions, there was a big price on her head. The Turks had boasted that, when they found Hatun, they were going to tear her limbs from her body and put them on display. All Armenian women who remained in Marash were to report to police headquarters so the Turks could identify Hatun. Before this, the women frantically smeared mud on Hatun's hair and rubbed charcoal on her face. They made her wear the tattered and bloodied clothing of a dead woman. Thankfully, she was not found out. She escaped but would, in small ways, carry that terror with her all of her days. We all shared our gut-wrenching experiences and remarkably were able to laugh through our tears.

Ferideh and her husband had a family of their own, all young adults. Charlie was the youngest, George the handsomest, and Edward the nicest and the only one of their boys who would talk to me man-to-man. The daughter of the family was Eleanor. I felt sorry for Eleanor, because she always seemed to have arguments with her mother. Maybe it was because she could never come up to her mother's exacting standards of behavior. Eleanor smoked, liked her alcohol, wore flashy clothes, and stayed up very late. As far as I knew, she also couldn't care less about going to church.

Evelyn and I learned much later that Jim had been exasperated by his wife's puritanical ways. With his money and standing in the community, he would have preferred to have Ferideh spend more time and money on her appearance instead of looking dowdy before her time. He wanted a woman who was beautiful to look at instead of someone who cared so little about outside appearances. There were rumors that he looked outside of the marriage for that kind of woman and broke Ferideh's heart. To compensate, she doted on her children, giving in to all of their demands for material things and basically spoiling them.

I could see early on that working in the packinghouse was a job with no future for me. I worked there for exactly one week. I left Evelyn and the children with Auntie Ferideh and came back up to San Francisco.

Luckily for me, there was an Armenian who owned Kasper's Hot Dogs, in Oakland, across the bay from San Francisco. He needed someone to take care of the business. I got the job, and as soon as I did, I brought my family to be with me. We rented an apartment at 100 Pierce Street at the corner of Waller in San Francisco. My brother-in-law Toros and his wife rented an apartment nearby at 96 Waller Street.

The Second World War brought with it more advantages for employment. I left Kasper's and was hired at the shipyard in Richmond, California, where I worked in the prefabrication shop. During the war, I also worked at the Bethlehem Steel Shipyard at Hunter's Point. I slept at home during the day and worked at night.

On July 23, 1943, another child was born to our family. Janet Anahid was a perfectly beautiful girl.

With so much money coming in, Evelyn spent much of her time at the produce markets shopping. It got so that my father-in-law, Hagop, was afraid that she would spend all the money I was making. He took her to a bank where, even though he could not speak one word of English, and very little Armenian, told her, in Turkish, to immediately open a savings account. She did!

Hagop was a shrewd man and encouraged all of his children to invest in property in America. He saw financial opportunities everywhere. His family, under the tutelage of his father, Toros, had, before the Marash War of 1920, extensive holdings in Marash, including a vineyard outside of the city and property that he rented out. The family tannery was famous because his father, Toros, had perfected the European style of making leather. The leather produced in their factory was superior to that of all of the other tanneries in Marash. The Turkish government confiscated their tannery and all of their property when Hagop was forced to leave (there were fifty gold pounds on his head) with the retreating French in the winter of 1920. But that is another story to be told.

Auntie Ferideh, with a group of Armenians, even went to Washington in the 1940s to petition the Turkish ambassador regarding the properties of their respective families in Turkey, to absolutely no avail. By confiscating

Armenian buildings, lands, and wealth, the Turkish middle class was created. That was one of the objectives behind the genocide.

After the war, Kasper Koojoolian the owner of Kasper's Hot Dogs on Telegraph Avenue in Oakland, California, asked me to work for him, managing the place, but I turned it down. That was a mistake that I regret to this day. I took odd jobs after the war years. I worked in the Texas Chili restaurant on Market Street in San Francisco owned by Ishkouhi and Gevan Manougian, but that didn't last long, and I even worked as a janitor in a movie theater.

With the money Evelyn saved, we were able to put a down payment on a two-story Victorian flat on Seventeenth Street between Noe and Sanchez Streets in San Francisco. This was a classic Victorian built in 1879. My brother-in-law Puzant hired me to work in his paint store on Market Street. Bay City Paint Company was famous, because for years the artists at the San Francisco Art Institute would buy their oil paints from him, cementing his reputation as one of the premier color mixers in the entire Bay Area. My job there was to deliver paints to customers.

When it came time for me to apply for citizenship, I told the judge that I didn't know the date of my birth. He told me that from that day on, it would be January 20, the day our presidents in America are inaugurated.

On September 9, 1947, our youngest child, Lucille Catherine, was born. She brought us so much happiness. My sister-in-law Rebecca was married then but childless. She asked Evelyn to give her Lucy, as she would have loved to have her for a daughter. But we couldn't part with her.

In my mid-fifties, I quit working for Bay City Paint Company. I didn't see much of a future there for me. But what could I do? It was a very tough time for me. I was rudderless and floundering around. Evelyn always told me that she would support me in whatever I wanted to do. I knew my family was relieved when I quit my job, as I was taking my frustrations out on them.

In 1958, as luck would have it, a man by the name of Tom Humphrey was selling his business, Bauer Paint Store, at 1376 Haight Street. Running the store was not his main occupation, because he worked full time as a fireman. I bought the store from Mr. Humphrey, as I had to do something to earn money. It was in the heart of the Haight-Ashbury district of San Francisco. I owned the business until 1982, when I retired. My daughter Janet was always good in math and she did my books until she moved to New York City.

I made friends with a small group of Armenians who belonged to Saint Gregory Armenian Church. We played pinochle at the Armenian club that was located around the block from the store. The Haight was a very interesting and troubled neighborhood in those days, with many lost souls wandering the streets. There were many stories all waiting to be told. I think I convinced some young people with whom I spoke to go back to their parents. I hope so.

I really enjoyed the visits of my friends to the store: Leo Lebedeff, Carl Zekarian, Walter Monina, Hazel Wood, Sam Jevarian, Sam Cousnar, Valerius Lubawin, and my closest friend, Khoushbul Khoushboulian. I rented the small unit in the back of the store to a single Armenian lady by the name of Efgeen. One day I found Khoushbul and Efgeen locked in an embrace. It happens!

Khoushbul was like a brother to me. He had a measured approach to life, and I appreciated his good advice. When he was dying from cancer, I visited him in the hospital for the last time. After the visit, I almost got killed crossing the street. I was in such reverie thinking about my friend that I didn't see a car that was turning the corner.

During my years as the proprietor of Bauer Paint Store, my wife, Evelyn, began to work as a seamstress at the New Method Laundry that was down a block from our house on Seventeenth Street. She worked there until it closed."

The Route Taken

Train:
Mosul to Baghdad

Cargo Ship:
Baghdad to Karachi
Karachi Hotel, India, 20 days

Cargo Ship:
Karachi to Bombay
Bombay, 2 months

Passenger Ship:
MS Boschfontein
Ceylon
Colombo
Indonesia
Singapore
Philippines
Hawaii
San Francisco
Arrived August 16, 1941

CHAPTER 14

CHOJUKNER, CHILDREN OF DELI SARKIS AND EVELYN

San Francisco, 1953. Picture taken in Auntie Rebecca and Uncle Arthur's garden. Left to right: Sarkis, Janet, Arthur, Ellen, Lucy, and our mother Evelyn.

I'D LIKE TO INTERJECT MY OWN OPINIONS HERE about what it was like growing up with parents who had endured so much and in many ways were deprived of normal childhoods. They both had to grow up real fast and assume responsibilities way beyond their years. I don't remember my mother, Evelyn, and my father, Sarkis, referring to any of us as *manoog*, which is the Armenian word for child. I do remember that they used the Turkish word for child, *cocuk*, while adding the Armenian ending "ner," making it *cocukner*, a composite word.

There were four of us cocukner. My father barely survived the genocide, and my mother and her family prepared to be deported three times in 1915 before the authorities told them they would not be deported, as they needed my grandfather's skills as a tanner. How nerve-wracking! She was deeply affected by what she heard, which were the screams of people being burned alive in a church, and of the murder of her aunt, Shamiram, and family during the Marash War of 1920. I fully intend to write about my mother's story another time.

My brother Arthur (Art) and I were born eighteen months apart. We were best buddies from childhood until our teen years. We'd go to the movies at the Castro Theatre, which was a few blocks from our house.

We loved comic books and poured over the hundreds that we owned. Oftentimes, we would trade our books for different ones with the neighborhood boys. We practiced drawing by copying the pictures. Art could really draw fighter planes down to the most intricate details, while I would design fashions for the comic-book character Tillie the Toiler. But, my favorite character in all of the comic books was Wonder Woman. She fought evil all over the universe and saved her mother and siblings from terrible predicaments. Maybe that's why I also loved the series of fairy tales by Andrew Lang, known as the *Fairy Books of Many Colors*. I craved stories in which the heroine was given almost insurmountable tasks to overcome. At the end of these stories I felt as if I had accomplished myself what the fictional character had done so well, which gave me so much satisfaction.

I also loved school. My younger sister Jan and her girlfriends became my students as I playacted being a teacher. So, after graduating from Mission High School, I went to San Francisco State College and earned a BA and then my teaching credential. I majored in social studies and minored in English. Later on, I earned a Ryan Single Subject Credential in Art. I taught for forty-two years in the San Francisco Unified School district, teaching in junior high schools, middle schools, a continuation high school, and comprehensive high schools. I loved teaching. I also enjoyed creating art, and through the years, I have spent hours drawing, painting, and printmaking. My work is in many private collections. For over a decade, I have been affiliated with Pacific Art League in Palo Alto and San Francisco Women Artists. If I had to start over, I would still choose teaching as my career.

After graduating from Mission High School, my brother attended City College of San Francisco, where he received his AA degree in mechanical drawing. He was a senior instrumentation designer/piping designer/electrical detailer and worked for more than twenty-five years for a large variety of engineering companies in the San Francisco Bay Area, specializing in oil refinery and chemical plant design and modification, and nuclear and fossil fuel power plant design and existing plant improvement modification, including the new BART station electrical construction. Arthur was also an accomplished photographer and an avid supporter of Armenian writers and artists, giving them not only moral but also financial support. He's the only one of us cocukner who had any children, two sons, Randy and Darryl Sarkis. He loved and cared deeply for them both.

Sadly, Art died of ALS (Lou Gehrig's disease) in 2007. He had a difficult time growing up, as my father was hardly ever there for him emotionally. My brother desperately needed his encouragement and support. He didn't get it. My mother, however, was very protective of Art and loved him unconditionally. Both Lucy and I cared for him in the last weeks of his life. Some months after his death, our mother, Evelyn, appeared to Lucy in a dream. She thanked Lucy for looking after our brother. Many people will miss Art. His friendships lasted over fifty years, attesting to his loyalty and love.

The middle child of the four of us was my sister Janet, aka Jan. I remember her as a little girl helping the ladies of the neighborhood with their household chores, cleaning their homes and shopping for them, so she could earn money. She said she also wanted to see how other people lived. A funny anecdote was when she would drink the Turkish coffee that our father prepared before she went to school and was so wired up from the caffeine that a teacher noticed and told her to stop drinking it. Sadly, in high school she hit a wall with my parents regarding her clothes, her hairdo, and her attitude (angry most of the time). This led to a total breakdown in communication with her mother and father. She spent a great deal of time not speaking to anyone on the home front. I felt sorry for everyone. When she did speak, she emphatically said that she was going to move out. My father told her she could do that, but first she would have to graduate from Mission High School and show him her diploma.

She graduated in the fall of 1960 and moved out of the house. While in high school, she met art student Robert Duran, who was studying at the San Francisco Art Institute. They moved in together. But, in 1963 she went to Hollywood, California, and rented an apartment on La Cienega Boulevard. She wanted to see if she could make it on her own. It didn't work out, and she moved back to San Francisco. Jan and Robert decided to go to New York City, as that's where many artists gravitated in order to become recognized and get their work into influential galleries. Jan wholeheartedly encouraged Bob's path as an artist and financially supported the two of them. She worked nights as a waitress at the Lion's Head Cafe next to the place made famous by the riots in the gay community—Stonewall.

After ten or more years of being together, Duran broke up with Jan. The split devastated her. He gave her a considerable amount of money, which enabled her to travel around the world. She went to Afghanistan (before the Soviet invasion) and Iran (while the Shah was in power). When she ran out of money, she worked as a chambermaid. Eventually she returned to New York and continued working as a waitress, but the job was causing her stress and recurring bad dreams. She quit and moved back to San Francisco, which made her parents very happy.

Jan studied at Ms. Marty's Beauty School and got her license. She worked at a number of salons before she opened her own business in the mid 1990s. All of her hard work finally paid off—her salon was the crowning achievement of her life. Her clients were devoted to her: some were with her for thirty-five years and even brought their children to her salon for haircuts. Many became loyal friends.

Besides working as a stylist, Jan painted in watercolors, which showed her talent as a budding artist, and took many stunning photographs on her travels around the world. Jan died two months short of her seventieth birthday on May 18, 2013, from complications of amyloidosis. She will be sorely missed by all who knew and loved her.

My youngest sister, Lucy, after graduating from Mission High School, went to City College of San Francisco and earned her AA degree in merchandising. For years she worked in the financial district doing various secretarial jobs. But her true skills were in altering fashion. She would buy a piece of clothing in a consignment shop and then, with trim, fabric, buttons, and her own innate skills, transform the item into a work of art. I believe she inherited her talents from my mother, Evelyn, my maternal grandmother, Hiranoush, and my paternal great-grandmother, Iscouhi. All were superb seamstresses. Lucy has gone to Al-Anon meetings for years because of the alcoholism of my father and has also become a lauded speaker and is very active in Toastmasters.

My parents loved all of us deeply. But they were just not very demonstrative. There were hugs and kisses and expressions of affection when we were babies and very young but little as we grew older, when we really could have used them. Heaven forbid that they should brag about us to anyone. They both were superstitious and felt the power of the evil eye. If they showed too much pride, they thought the evil eye would work its insidious power and ruin what was good. They did not want to take that chance.

Once, my father announced to all of us, "I love you kids very much!" We were struck dumb and very surprised. In retrospect, I think life would have been so much easier for all of us growing up if both Mother and Father had been more outgoing with affection and had not kept all their good thoughts about us to themselves.

4-1248

No. 146566

Amount $ 7100.00

POLICY OF TITLE INSURANCE

CITY TITLE INSURANCE COMPANY

68 Sutter Street

SAN FRANCISCO

CALIFORNIA

ISSUED TO

SARKIS SARKISIAN and EVELYN
SARKISIAN, his wife, and
THE SAN FRANCISCO BANK,
a California corporation

Dated

July 30, 1946

FORM 43 7500 9-45

Title to the Victorian flats at 3873 and 3875 Seventeenth Street, San Francisco, California, purchased in 1946 for $7,100.

Ellen remembers the day that her parents finally owned their Victorian flats free and clear. That night her mother, Evelyn, gathered her children on the floor of the dining room with its impossibly high ceiling. They made imaginary Armenian delicacies, pretending to roll out the dough and filling it with sweetmeats and then folding up the pastry to start again. Ellen will never forget her mother's happiness that night.

CHAPTER 15

SUPPRESSED
MEMORIES AND
HIDDEN HISTORY

*The illustration on the currency, designed by Arshak
Fetvadjian, depicts a woman with a Jayr (spinning
wheel) on the left and a Nazoog (reel) on the right.*

SOMETIMES SUPPRESSED MEMORIES JUMP OUT AT THE STRANGEST TIMES. In looking back at my father's life and experiences, one incident really stands out. I was a child at the time.

Our family loved to go to parades. They were festive occasions that celebrated our patriotic spirit and love of America, our country. On this particular day, I was standing next to my father on Market Street, which starts at the Ferry Building in San Francisco. I don't remember the theme of the parade. I do know that as one group stopped in front of us, my father grew visibly agitated and began talking loudly and swearing. The Shriners and their drum corps had paused momentarily right next to us. We could almost touch them. They were dressed in voluminous black pants and small red vests. Perched ever so conspicuously on their heads were red fezzes with long, black tassels. They looked like Turks.

One of the drummers, a corpulent, olive-skinned man with a large kettledrum strapped to his body, was sweating profusely. His attention so focused on the group leader some distance away that he missed the vitriol being spewed in his direction by my father. I was afraid that at any moment my father was going to leap out of the spectator section and begin pummeling the drummer. What a relief when the Shriners began moving.

The second episode happened many years later. I had taken my father to a carpet gallery in San Francisco, which was headlining the weavers and carpets from a village in Turkey. The young female villagers would take turns sitting in front of a loom and would demonstrate the process of weaving. I encouraged my father to speak to them in Turkish. He hadn't spoken the language for years, as all of our relatives who spoke it had died.

He began talking with one of the weavers, asking her if she was married or single, and other similar, friendly questions. She answered smiling, and the conversation, I'm sure, would have continued in that lighthearted manner. But, suddenly he looked down to see a very old spinning wheel. His expression changed from quizzical to very dark and distressed. Eyes wide and no longer smiling, he said in Armenian, "Get me out of here! Now!" I hurriedly ushered him out the door.

I could have asked him about the object that had so upset him, but I didn't need to. My grandmother had owned a spinning wheel.

The third incident took place at Kelly Home that was on the twenty-second hundred block of Forty-eighth Avenue in San Francisco. That's where my father lived after my mother died. He had tried his best to live in the family house for five years following her death, but we could see, when he became ill, that he wasn't taking care of himself, and he was very lonely.

At Kelly Home, the caretakers, Candy and Mark Myers, looked after him and a number of other elderly people who lived there. They were a wonderful couple and saved my father's life in so many ways. Candy nursed him back to health when he caught terrible colds in the winter, and Mark took care of him mentally, talking with him and sharing a cigarette or two.

Mark had an Armenian connection. He had been married before to the daughter of the French-Armenian singer Charles Aznavour. When we met Mark, his ex-wife was living in Fresno and their teenaged daughter Seta came up from Fresno to visit. She had an outgoing, sunny personality like her father.

Mark was an accomplished musician and would play the piano at Kelly Home and sing for the residents, often asking them to join in. I learned from him about the song made famous by Charles Aznavour, "They Fell." It was about the deportations.

On one visit with my father, I told him of the book I was reading, *Hitler and the Armenian Genocide* by Kevork B. Bardakjian. In the book, the author recounts that in 1943, the remains of the man most instrumental in destroying the Armenians was returned to Turkey from Germany. At the end of the First World War, Talaat had escaped to Germany. He feared retribution from the victors, as Germany and Turkey lost the war, and revenge by the Armenians. He was assassinated by Soghomon Tehlirian, an Armenian genocide survivor, on March 13, 1921.

Bardakjian writes that it is unclear who negotiated in Turkey for the return of Talaat's body. However, Mustafa Ismet Inonu, the president of Turkey in 1943 (he assumed the position in 1938), was at one time a member of the Committee of Union and Progress. Inonu was also an avid supporter of Talaat's inhumane policies towards Turkey's minorities.

Examples would be the massacre of the Kurds and hidden Armenians in Dersim in the 1930s and the draconian taxes imposed on Armenians, Greeks, and Jewish minorities in the early 1940s.

I told my father about what happened to the remains of Talaat once he was returned to Turkey. The respect and praise heaped upon the monster deeply upset him. A special mausoleum had been prepared for him and he was interred with much pomp, circumstance, and high military honors. The place of internment is the Monument of Liberty (Abide-i-Hurriyet), located on a high hill in the Caglayan district of Istanbul.

My father was speechless, which was unusual, as he never ever was at a loss for words in whatever language he knew. He stared ahead and took a long, deep drag on his cigarette and said ironically, "Well, this monument for Talaat Pasha should be a very good place for all of the pigeons in Istanbul to fly over and take a shit!"

In 1996, the remains of Enver Pasha (1881–1922) were brought back to Turkey from Tajikistan, where he had been killed in the 1920s. He had vehemently hated all Armenians and the other Christian minorities, which included the Greeks and the Assyrians. On August 5, 1996, there was a state funeral for him, and his remains were buried in a newly built tomb that was next to that of Talaat. He was treated like a hero, whereas in reality he, too, had been a brutal fascist. It is a disgrace to honor such men.

How does one reconcile mass murder to the concept of heroism? Wouldn't the world be outraged if the remains of Hitler and Goebbels had been interred in a specially created mausoleum in the center of the city of Berlin? On top of that, be given overwhelmingly positive accolades for their actions? The outrage would be deafening. Not so for the internment of the mass murderers in Turkey. So few people across the globe have even heard of the Young Turks and their actions, and those who have heard and try to do something about it are subjected to harassment on a governmental level.

With a coterie of so-called historians backing them up, successive governments in Turkey have kept up the façade of "It was a civil war!" for the shameful events that the Young Turks perpetrated so many decades ago. They will not acknowledge that the genocide actually happened. In Turkey, harassment and murder of Armenians continue to this day. Why are only sixty thousand Armenians remaining in Turkey? At one time, Armenians made up 20 percent of the population. The answer is that Armenians and other Christians are still treated as second-class citizens, and those that can, leave.

In the Armenian schools in Istanbul, only the Turkish version of history is taught, in which the events of 1915 are virtually ignored. Armenian priests need metal detectors at their churches because of the threats of extremists. The Turkish-Armenian newspaper *AGOS* receives a steady stream of abusive e-mails daily by Turkish nationalists.

In the so-called enlightened country of Turkey, Hrant Dink, the Armenian editor of *AGOS*, was murdered outside of his office: two bullets to the head and two bullets to his body. The crime took place on January 19, 2007. In the words of the great journalist Robert Fisk, "Hrant Dink was a man who tried to create a dialogue between Turks and Armenians to help them reach a common narrative of the 20th century's first holocaust." Just as the Turkish police stood proudly next to Hrant Dink's alleged murderer after his arrest, so the current government of Turkey stands proudly next to the record of Talaat and the Young Turks. Woe to those who try to change the official narrative of the Turkish state.

In 1989, Aristide D. Caratzas published the book *The Slaughterhouse Province: An American Diplomat's Report on the Armenian Genocide 1915–1917* in New Rochelle, New York. Leslie A. Davis was the U.S. Consul in Harput during the years 1915–1917. Susan K. Blair, a historian and researcher, came upon Consul Davis's report seven decades after he had sent it to the State Department. She saw how important it was, and after editing the report and writing a superb introduction, she showed it to a publisher who turned it down for publication, fearful of controversy. The book did find its publisher in Aristide D. Caratzas.

Even before it was published, trouble started. Word got out about the discovery of the long-lost documents and the forthcoming publication. Then the harassment began. There was a bomb threat. Consequently, law enforcement and security experts were called in to investigate. Ms. Blair and her family went into hiding.

During the massacres and deportations of the entire population of Armenians living in the Ottoman Empire, Talaat insisted that absolutely no photographs were to be taken of the deportees. There was also to be no help given whatsoever: no food, water, or medical attention. Leslie A. Davis managed to take pictures, knowing he would be in great danger if found out. Some even appear in *The Slaughterhouse Province*. They are faded, but remain as witness to the events that took place.

The Turkish government was outraged at the appearance of this book in 1989, and the fact that the world was now going to be privy to the events they had been trying so mightily to cover up. When Ms. Blair was doing her research in the National Archives, she noted the following: "Volumes of records from the American Embassy in Constantinople from 1915 had been looted. The entire section devoted to social problems in the Ottoman Turkish Empire in 1915, which would cover the Armenian genocide, has been cut out of the bound volume leaving only stubs of pages. The rolls of microfilm covering the massacre of Armenians and Assyrians in northwestern Persia during the Turkish invasions of the area during World War I disappeared from the Archives' Microfilm Reading Room."[10]

The Turkish fairy tale continues, with the narrative being that the Turks were helpless victims and the Armenians, the perpetrators. To establish such a narrative solidly and make certain it was entrenched, the government had to do a number of things. First, a complete break with the Ottoman past had to take place. When the Turkish Republic was created in 1923 and Ataturk came to power, he knew language was the key to reinforcing his break with the past. Very few people could read the alphabet with its Arabic script. How perfect for Ataturk and his plan to create a new society from scratch. He called on the Armenian expert on the Turkish language, Hagop Martayan, who had been born in Turkey in 1895, graduated from Robert College in 1915, and was at that time living in Bulgaria.

Martayan, in the 1930s, replaced the Ottoman script with a phonetic variant of the Latin. It was now possible for many more people to learn how to read. Ataturk also changed the man's name to Dilacar, which means "tongue opener" in Turkish, making it impossible for many in that country to know that an Armenian had transformed their language. All Persian and Arabic vocabulary were at the same time removed.

Continuing on in the 1930s and inspired by Ataturk, educators created a new Turkish identity. The Turkish race became the mother of all races while the Turkish language became the "mother tongue of all other languages." According to these educational theorists, the Turks appeared very far back in the history of Anatolia in "the form of the Hittites" and not in the latter half of the eleventh century, as they in truth appeared in eastern Anatolia.[11] Ayfer, who with her husband, Mazhar, and tour guide Armen Aroyan had accompanied me to my father's village, laughingly spoke of her Hittite ancestors.

After the collapse of the Young Turk regime in 1918, the head of security, Aziz Bey, quickly destroyed the archives of the special organization, Teshkilat-Mahsusa. This contemptible arm of the government of Talaat had been established in 1914. Many of its members had been recruited in prisons and "in the gutter" to carry out the orders of the government.[12] Their function was comparable to that of the SS in Nazi Germany.

Zohrap Krikorian, who was born in Istanbul in 1916 and died in San Francisco in 2007, was a famous bicyclist who had traveled 55,000 miles around the world in the years 1959–1962. On his bicycle trip he visited Robert College in Istanbul where Araxie's second husband, Missak Israelian, had been a professor of literature. Araxie said that he had been killed by firing squad in 1918.

While at Robert College, Zohrap asked to see the archives in order to get information about his father. The archivist at the college told Zohrap to wait so that he could search for his father's records. Zohrap waited for hours. Finally the man returned and told him that no records of his father could be found.

Turkish students have been told for generations how lucky they are to be Turks. But they haven't been told the truth about their history. Instead, a truly reprehensible video, entitled *Blonde Bride* and developed by the Turkish military, is part and parcel of the curriculum in the schools. In it, Armenians are horrific monsters brutalizing the helpless Turkish population in the 1915 era. Street names and schools are named after the criminals of the past, all made out to be national heroes. I'm very skeptical about any changes happening as long as Prime Minister Recep Erdogan stands alongside Omar al-Bashir, Sudan's leader, and proudly states that Muslims do not commit genocide.

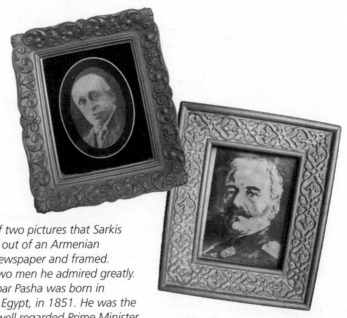

Left: One of two pictures that Sarkis lovingly cut out of an Armenian language newspaper and framed. These are two men he admired greatly. Boghos Nubar Pasha was born in Alexandria, Egypt, in 1851. He was the son of the well regarded Prime Minister of Egypt Nubar Pasha (known as Abu Falah—the father of the peasants). Boghos Nubar was the chairman of the Armenian National Assembly, and with ten other Armenians founded the Armenian General Benevolent Union (AGBU) in Cairo, Egypt, on April 15, 1906. He died in Paris in 1930.

Right: Framed photo of Andranik Ozanian (known famously as General Andranik). Born in Sebinkarahisar, the Ottoman Empire, on February 25, 1865, he died on August 31, 1927, in Richard Springs, California. He was an Armenian military commander and greatly admired as a national hero.

CHAPTER 16

THE SCARS
HE CARRIED

Deli Sarkis seated in the living room of his daughter Ellen and son-in-law Glen's home in San Francisco in the late 1980s. He looks at peace with himself.

THE SCAR ON THE TOP OF MY FATHER'S HEAD was a puckered-up jagged line, like a wayward tributary of a mighty river. Near the scar was a square indentation, a half an inch in diameter, that was actually evidence of a bayonet entry. When we were younger, he would tell us his story of escape from Basmakhanien station. Then, Father would pull up his pant leg and show us the other scar where the bayonet had also entered. He was, according to my Aunt Rebecca, a "Leftover of the Sword," a derogatory term used to designate a survivor of the genocide. In my father's case, he was someone forever haunted by memories of the dead and dying. I wonder now whether he must have felt guilt at having survived. Was that why he could never really enjoy life and realize how lucky he was with such a wonderful wife and loving children?

When we were growing up, his rages would come and go. Sometimes he would be so understanding and speak so softly and sweetly, like the father we always dreamed about. At other times he would be very critical of us all and beside himself with anger. I tried to understand, but could never discover the reason for this split personality. It made for a very uncertain existence because, from day to day, we did not know how he would behave. To me, he was the master and commander of the torpedo station, blasting those who loved and cared for him deeply, as we all did. But he continued to carve big chunks out of the good feelings we had for him, seemingly oblivious to how he was hurting us all.

However, in the midst of the oceanic turmoil of our daily lives, there were islands of respite and happiness. In the 1950s, besides the family gatherings around the television set, my father and I would watch the Friday night fights together. We would cheer on our favorite boxers, among the greatest middleweights in boxing history: Carmen Basilio, Florentino Fernandez, Benny "Kid" Peret, Kid Gavilan, Rocky Castellani, and Pierre Langlois. We very much enjoyed our boxing nights and the camaraderie we shared.

After her operation in the early 1950s, Mom organized a camping trip to Clear Lake, California. While there, Dad pitched a tent and Mom cooked on a little camp stove. We kids had an absolute blast, exploring the environs, meeting new friends, and creating memories. My teenaged brother caused a sensation at a rock-and-roll party, dancing with a much older woman, much to the delight of my sisters, Janet and Lucy.

Most of the time Dad sat around bare-chested, catching the rays of the sun and seemingly at a loss as to what to do. We pleaded with our mother to please, please tell him to wear an undershirt, as he was so hairy. It was positively embarrassing to look at the long, luxurious hair growing out of his back.

This leads me to our trips to the San Francisco Zoo during that same period in our lives. Every other Sunday, or so it seemed, Dad would announce, "Let's go and visit our relatives at the zoo." By that he meant Monkey Island. When we got there, we would stand by him and observe "our relatives" grooming one another, or watching us, or tending to their young. There was absolutely no doubt in our minds, after seeing our father in the flesh and in full hairy mode, that those tiny, playful creatures on that man-made island across the moat from us were truly our relatives.

Another favorite place to visit on Sundays was Playland at the Beach. At that time, it was a ramshackle amusement park, now long gone but fondly remembered. Dad would head for his favorite gambling concession, while we children and Mom were left to our own devices. That was no problem. We got on rides, went into a house of mystery and enchantment with mirrors that distorted our bodies and faces, rode a slide that went on for a mile, sat on a large spinning device that would turn ever faster as we would fly off, rode giant tea cups, or climbed into racing cars and drove mercilessly while bumping other vehicles. It was a lot of fun! One memorable afternoon, Dad even went on the roller coaster by himself, just for the experience. We would swear, later, that he looked positively green as the roller coaster inched its way up to the heights before its speedy descent.

In the mid 1960s, three of us had already moved out of the house and were on our own. Lucy, my youngest sister, was the only one remaining at home with our parents. She experienced father's illness and the despair of my mother firsthand. The alcoholism was not easy on my father, my mother, or my sister. Looking back now I know that his drinking started when he took over Bauer Paint Store from Tom Humphrey, who was an alcoholic himself encouraging my father to join him for a drink or two. It didn't take very long for my father to become addicted.

Finally, my mother's health broke, worn down by years of trying to cope with the disease of alcoholism and ridden with stress. She suffered a heart attack. It was a serious one and put over half of her heart out of commission. I was angry with her for not moving out years before, or at least trying to seek help through Alcoholics Anonymous. It is not disloyal to seek help for yourself. For almost three years, she struggled with a very badly damaged heart. On the evening before the day she died, I called her at the hospital, not knowing how near the end of her life she was. But when I spoke with her and heard how she could barely talk due to the lack of air to her lungs, I realized it was too late. I told her that I was on my way, but she told me not to come.

Her doctor notified my father very early in the morning about her condition. He hurriedly dressed and rushed over to her side. He was with her, gently holding her hand for a long time. Then he told her he wanted to have a cigarette in the lobby. She told him not to go. "I'm right here, Evelyn," he replied, "I won't leave you!" She took a final, labored breath and died. It was January 1983. His companion, his best friend, lover, and wife, was gone.

Her funeral was packed with relatives and friends who truly loved her. Lucy told me that when she had gone over to the house afterwards, it was filled with flowers from the floor to the ceiling in every room. My poor father was wandering around like a lost soul. Finally he pulled himself together and told Lucy in a commanding voice, "Get these flowers out of here!" She did, donating some of the more beautiful bouquets to various churches.

Thinking back now, I can see why my parents were so bound together. When she first met him, he dazzled her. He was good looking, always kept a wad of money in his pocket, articulated beautifully, and wouldn't take guff from anybody. He was a strong, forthright man, so different from her, with her gentle ways and reticence to speak up for herself. It was only much later, when he was in the throes of alcoholism, that she became the strong one and took care of household matters. However, she appreciated the fact that he went to his paint store everyday. Even though he didn't make a lot of money, he didn't sit around the house. She worked at New Method Laundry, a block away from their home. She was a seamstress and told me that her job literally saved her life. Between the two of them and her skills at budgeting, they led a comfortable life.

I have often wondered what he would have accomplished if he did not have so many insecurities behind his outward blustery personality. He was a linguistic sponge, soaking up languages wherever he lived, and he did so very quickly. His life depended on it. He spoke Turkish, Armenian, Greek, Bulgarian, Arabic, Kurdish, Farsi, and English. He was a wonderful cook and a terrific gardener. What a splendid garden my mother and he created together: the gorgeous, sweet-smelling roses, the lemon tree, the olive tree, and all the herbs that she used in her cooking.

He liked to transform found objects. Oftentimes, when he owned the paint store on Haight Street, he would bring home discarded household items that were left on the sidewalks of the neighborhood. You could always find my father either in their garden or working on a project on the old oak counter that extended the full length of the basement. He would strip wooden objects to their natural state and then apply coat after coat of varnish until you could see your own reflection in them.

The back stairs of our Victorian residence were falling apart. We were afraid to walk up and down on them as they would sway from side to side with every step. Finally my father convinced a friend to help him and together they tore down the stairs and put up new ones. Remarkably, those stairs lasted for over forty years.

He had a keen sense of history and was thoroughly cognizant of current events. During the height of the McCarthy hearings, the Bay Area Armenian community congregated in a huge hall for a presentation and movie. It was a propaganda film depicting Joseph Stalin as a benign and loveable figure. My father stood up suddenly and told all of us to get up because were leaving the hall immediately. It could have been, as I think back, he feared the hall would be raided by Senator Joseph McCarthy, and we'd all end up in jail.

When I was a child, my father was my hero. I don't remember this incident but he certainly did, as it was a memorable event for him. The two of us were in a movie theater watching the film in which a dog was being abused. My father saw that I was very upset. Finally, I had enough and I stood up and said, in a very loud voice, "Daddy, save that dog!" My father said the audience erupted in sympathetic laughter.

During the Second World War, when he worked at the Hunter's Point Naval Shipyard, our little family was on a streetcar going to the christening of a newly built ship. My mother and father were sitting together and Arthur and I were sitting across from them. Periodically I would turn and gaze at him. I was so proud of him sitting there, wearing his yellow hard hat. I have no doubt that I thought he built the entire ship himself.

In the early 1970s, the Armenian Missionary Association of America sponsored a tour for its members to the Middle East and Armenia. I don't know how she did it, but my mother convinced my father to join her on this adventure. Mother regularly donated to the AMAA and was looking forward to seeing all of the places on the tour. She was also pleased that one of the tour leaders was the Reverend Giragos H. Chopourian, at that time the head of the association.

When the group stopped in Istanbul, a site on the itinerary was the orphanage that the association sponsored. My father told my mother that he would not go inside, because it would have been too hard for him to see the orphans. Instead, he walked around Istanbul and looked at different sites, even removing his slacks and wading into the Bosporus.

Mother related that, while there in the orphanage, the visitors were treated to a lovely meal consisting of chicken and other hearty fare while the orphans were given some kind of gruel. The group, including my mother, was outraged and complained so loudly that all of a sudden there was enough chicken for the children also.

On another occasion, my father and mother ventured out together without the other members of their group. They selected a nice restaurant, and when they went inside and spoke to the young proprietor in Turkish, he was so impressed by their impeccable Turkish that the meal was served with the compliments of the house. When, in answer to his questions, they told him about their ancestry, they realized, sadly, that the young man knew nothing of the Armenians who had been the native population in Turkey for over three thousand years. Turkish was the first language that all Armenian children were taught, and that's why my parents knew the language so well. After the meal, they told the young man how appreciative they were of his kind hospitality and delicious food.

On this same trip, they visited my father's second cousin, Egsapet Baharyan. It was a very sentimental and sweet time that the two cousins shared. My mother took a picture of them together.

When their tour group went to Armenia, on the last leg of the journey, both my mother and father were very impressed by what they saw. They absolutely loved the water and wrote back home that they would drink the water right out of the water fountains. My mother said that the bread was absolutely the most delicious she had ever eaten. The fact that everywhere they went they heard Armenian spoken made both of them even happier. My father spent some time sitting in the lobby of the Hotel Ani, hoping that someone who knew him from the old days would recognize him. That didn't happen.

When it was time for the last banquet, in Yerevan, the capital of Armenia, each member of the group was encouraged to stand and say something about Armenia. My mother said that my father was particularly eloquent that evening giving the assembled group a capsule history of the Armenian experience since 1915, when our people were the pitiful remnants of a destroyed culture, wandering the world searching for a home, while desperately clinging to our language and everything that had made us so unique as a people. He said that the journey from that abject privation and destitution to this, our homeland, made him so proud. He continued by noting that when he and his wife went to the museums, monasteries, and churches and heard the lilting sounds of Armenian spoken everywhere, he knew we were alive and well as a people and a culture.

My mother came from a family of men and women who were talented and hard working, but did not have a flair for language. She told me that my father did, and was a wonderful storyteller besides. How often, she remembered, our relatives and his trucker friends in Mosul doubled over in laughter as he recounted the experiences of the Turkish sage, Mullah Nasr ed-Din. Naturally, the funniest stories were often the off-color ones.

I found out that this talent came to him early on. In 1988, I received a reply to a letter I had sent to Bulgaria. It was from the daughters of my father's best friend from his boyhood days in the village of Keramet. Their mother, Hermine Sarkisian Ashirian, had been born in the village of Jerakh in the province of Bursa. Her family had gone to Bulgaria after the massacres and deportations, and while there she, at the age of twelve, saw my father. This would have been in 1923. Some of the deported Armenians had congregated in an Armenian elementary school in Rousse, and she recalled how my father would tell the assembled group about the massacres and deportations in vivid detail. She never forgot him or his accounts.

Years later, when he would meet his friends at the Armenian social hall for pinochle and conversation, the stories continued. The deacon of Saint Gregory Armenian Church at that time, Aris Balian, said that my father was the most interesting person he had encountered. He continued by saying that he was someone who would always have something riveting to talk about whenever the friends got together.

My father's stay at Kelly Home was nearing its end when the caretaker, Candy Myers, became pregnant. She was overjoyed with happiness, but Mrs. Kelly could not keep her in her condition, as all of the occupants were vulnerable elderly people. The situation became very nasty between Candy and Mrs. Kelly because Candy did not want to lose her job. Eventually, Kelly Home was no more.

The residents had to find other places to live. The move was not a good one for my father, as the caretakers of the next facility, run by Catholic nuns, could barely speak English and basically had no idea what they were doing. Unbeknownst to Lucy and me, my father was being overmedicated by his doctor. We found out soon enough when my father had a violent seizure at the home. The young, inexperienced caretakers became hysterical and were absolutely helpless. One of them finally had the good sense to call my sister Lucy and was blubbering on the phone. Lucy calmly told her to immediately call 911, which she did.

My father was taken by ambulance to the nearest facility, Seton Hospital in Daly City, not Kaiser Foundation, the hospital to which he belonged. Lucy called me and I rushed over and picked her up from her home. We were both nervous wrecks. It's a miracle that we reached the hospital without getting into an accident, as it was nighttime and I kept driving around in circles. When we got to Seton, the doctor in attendance met us and stated that our father, in the emergency room, was dying. I couldn't go in, as I was overcome with emotion and upset. Lucy did go in. I paced outside for at least five minutes and then asked myself, "How can I let my sister, Lucy, handle this all by herself?" So I went inside.

The doctor asked us, "Since your father is dying, do you girls want us to remove the respirator tube?" We assumed he knew what he was talking about, so we half-heartedly said "Yes." It was done. We sadly stood side by side, looking down at our father. At any moment we expected his life's energy to slowly ebb. Instead we both heard his breathing start to come back. Lucy nudged me and said that she heard him snoring. We started laughing and the doctor was stunned beyond belief. Just a few minutes earlier he had encouraged us to say a few words before his passing. I had refused to do that. Lucy then announced that our father, like the proverbial cat, did indeed have nine lives.

I wish I could say that Father recovered, but he didn't. Lucy and I ended up taking him to another convalescent facility in Millbrae. It was far from perfect, but it was so much better than the indescribable dungeons for the elderly that we had seen before we chose it.

Lucy and I both visited him as often as we could. Once, out of the blue, he blurted out to me, "I'll probably burn in hell!" Obviously, he was doing an inventory of his life and thinking of the hereafter. I didn't press him and ask why and what had he done that was so awful to make him think that way. His life was becoming harder, as he was now able to move about only in a wheelchair. He was also terrified of having another seizure.

It was during the last week of his life that my Aunt Arlene and her husband, my uncle Richard Kazarian, visited him. Later Aunt Arlene told me that my father was very sharp mentally. I already knew that from my visits.

How strange that I thought back to another story he told us. It was not about the Armenian genocide but about a man who at one time was a convict. His name was Jean Valjean and he was the main character in the great novel by Victor Hugo, *Les Miserables*. My father had not read the book but had seen the silent film based on the novel in Bulgaria. Years later, when he told his little children about it, we could tell how much he loved the character of Jean and now, in retrospect, I see how much he identified with the character.

My father died on April 19, 1995, just five days short of the eightieth anniversary of the Armenian genocide. None of his children were there at the time of his death. I rushed to the facility as soon as they notified me of his passing. He was laid out on the bed, looking so small and bird-like, not the powerful presence he had always been in life.

There was no Cosette and Marius to clasp his hands, no Shakeh, or Minas, or Janet, or Lucy to comfort him. There was no lilting French spoken in the halls of the facility, just Tagalog and Spanish. His last room was dark, with no window. Nor was there the beautiful light from the silver candlesticks that he had so memorably told us about when he spoke of the last moments of Jean Valjean's life.

But, like Jean Valjean, my father had found the redemption he wanted so much in his life in the love of his two daughters, Lucy and me. A long time ago, we had forgiven him for the difficulties of growing up with such a wounded, but at the same time such a vibrant and charismatic, human being. We knew that he would be forever in our hearts, and his story, along with that of our beloved relatives and the villagers of Keramet, would be with us also.

Yes, father, we will always hold fast to your words: "Keep moving" and "Never lose yourselves." We have kept moving and we have never lost ourselves. We know who we are, thanks to you.

Mosul, Iraq, 1939. Evelyn holding a cup. Left to right: Evelyn with her siblings: Edward, Evelyn, Arlene, Rebecca holding Ellen Shakeh, and Toros on right.

1939. Ellen Shakeh with puppy.

Aleppo, Syria, 1937. Toros and Arpine Shamlian. They traveled with Evelyn and Sarkis's family to America in 1941.

The clothing label from inside a very heavy black wool coat which Sarkis brought to America from Mosul. Ellen sent it to Armenia after the devastating earthquake on December 7, 1988. Dajod Andonian was Sarkis's tailor in Mosul.

Mosul, Iraq, 1934. Sarkis is holding some sort of portfolio.

Yosemite, California, 1941. Sarkis on trip to Yosemite with his wife's relatives.

Sarkis's small leather passport and important documents case.

Fresno, California, 1941. Ferideh Vagim (Evelyn's aunt) with her husband Jim Vagim. He owned a packinghouse.

Fresno, California, 1941. Back: unknown woman, unknown man, Hagop Shamlian, Toros Shamlian, Rebecca Shamlian, Jim Vagim, unknown, Sarkis, Ferideh Shamlian Vagim, and Hatun Bazarian. Front: Edward Shamlian, Eleanor Vagim, Hatun's daughter, Arlene Shamlian, and unknown girl.

Iraq. Minas Papazian, Ellen and Arthur's godfather, and the family left behind in Iraq. Ellen's picture is on the table.

San Francisco, 1941.
Arpine, Evelyn's sister-in-law on left and Evelyn on right with Ellen and Arthur sitting on wool rug.

San Francisco, 1943. Duboce Park, renamed by Ellen and Arthur "Kuzoom Park" (in honor of an elderly Armenian gentleman with whom Ellen and Arthur spoke fluent Armenian). Ellen standing and Arthur second from left in front row.

*San Francisco, 1949.
In the backyard of the
neighbor's house. Left
to right: Ellen, Jan, and
Arthur with Evelyn.*

*San Francisco, 1948. An evening at Puzant Shamlian and Viola's home. Left to right:
Evelyn, Jan, Arthur, Ellen, Sarkis with Lucy on his knee.*

San Francisco, late 1950s. Sarkis inside his paint store in the Haight Ashbury district.

San Francisco, late 1950s. Sarkis outside his paint store.

San Francisco, 1963. Evelyn and Sarkis's twenty-fifth wedding anniversary photo. Left to right, front row: Evelyn, Sarkis, and Lucy. Back row: Jan, Arthur, and Ellen.

Teacher Ellen Sarkisian.

Herbert Hoover Junior High School, San Francisco, 1970. Ellen organized the Medieval Pleasure Faire that was held in the library of the school. Some of Ellen's students who entertained the entire student body for the whole day.

San Francisco, 1971. Glen Earl Chesnut: Cowboy, merchant seaman, artist, writer, and husband of Ellen.

Concord, California, 1978. Left to right: Darryl Sarkis in arms of grandfather Sarkis and Randy with grandmother Evelyn.

Arthur Minas; draftsman, photographer, avid supporter of Armenian artists, writers, and Armenian causes. A good friend to many.

Concord, California, 1978. New father Arthur with baby Darryl Sarkis and Randy.

San Francisco, 2000. Darryl Sarkis.

San Francisco, 1966. The garden of Evelyn and Sarkis's Victorian flat on Seventeenth Street.

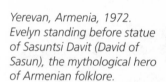

Yerevan, Armenia, 1972. Evelyn standing before statue of Sasuntsi Davit (David of Sasun), the mythological hero of Armenian folklore.

Istanbul, Turkey, 1972. Two cousins reunited, Egsapet and Sarkis.

San Francisco, 1994. Candy with baby daughter and husband Mark Myers, caretakers at Kelly Home. They really took care of Sarkis. He loved them both.

San Francisco, 1990. In front of Kelly Home. Glen (Ellen's husband), Ellen, Sarkis, and Lucille, the youngest child of the family.

San Francisco, 1982.
Jan Anahid Sarkisian.

New York City, mid 1970s.
Jan Anahid Sarkisian.

San Francisco, 1990. Ellen, Lucy, and Zohrap Krikorian, the famous bicyclist and world traveler.

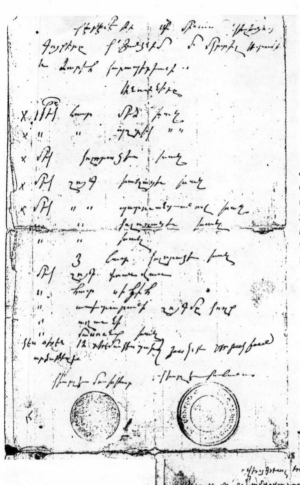

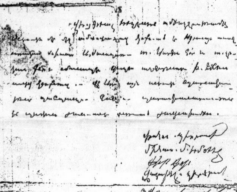

1918 list of the crosses and other valuables of Saint Minas Church (Keramet Village), stamped and notarized by the head of the village and signed by the Board of Trustees.

WORKS CITED

1. Tolegian, Aram. 1979. *Armenian Poetry Old and New*. Detroit, MI: Wayne State University Press.

2. Shannon, Ashley. 1999. *Irish Blessings*. Philadelphia, PA: Running Press Publishers.

3. Inan, Huri Islamoglu, Editor. 1987. *The Ottoman Empire and the World Economy*. UK: Cambridge University Press.

4. Mouradian, George. 1995. *Armenian InfoText*. Southgate, MI: Bookshelf Publishers.

5. Abrahamian, Levon, and Nancy Sweezy. 2001. *Armenian Folk Arts, Culture, and Identity*. Bloomington: Indiana University Press.

6. Abrahamian, Levon, and Nancy Sweezy. 2001. *Armenian Folk Arts, Culture, and Identity*. Bloomington: Indiana University Press.

7. Nalbandian, Inga. 2007. *Your Brother's Blood Cries Out*. Translated by Victoria Rowe. London: Gomidas Institute.

8. Sanson, Marie. June 2010 and August 2011. This quotation is from the recollections of Marie Sanson, now residing in Athens, Greece. Ms. Sanson was born in Corfu, on September 8, 1922, the date the Greeks commemorate as the anniversary of the "Great Catastrophe." I spoke with Ms. Sanson on the phone in June 2010 and again in August 2011. She said many people in Corfu were from Smyrna and the Southern Marmara region of Turkey. Ms. Sanson, long retired, was a secretary-typist in the office of the Consulate General of Greece on Gough Street in San Francisco.

9. Mouradian, George. 1995. *Armenian InfoText*. Southgate, MI: Bookshelf Publishers.

10. Davis, Leslie A. 1989. *The Slaughterhouse Province*. Edited by Susan K. Blair. New Rochelle, NY: Aristide D. Caratzas, Publisher.

11. Vryonis, Speros Jr. 2005. *The Mechanism of Catastrophe*. New York: Greekworks.com.

12. Derogy, Jacques. 1990. *Resistance and Revenge*. Translated by A. M. Berrett. New Brunswick, NJ and London: Transaction Publishers.

NOTES

Vartavar. One of the five main Armenian Church feast days celebrated in conjunction with the Transfiguration. Vartavar was an old heathen ritual celebrating the New Year that was August 1 by the Armenian calendar. Homage was paid to the goddess Asdghig by adorning her statue with a multitude of roses. After Armenia became a Christian state in 301, the Vartavar feast was replaced with the Transfiguration while still retaining the Vartavar name.

Hambardzum. Pagan festival related to marriage. The Hambardzum Festival, which marks the Ascension of Christ forty days after Easter, also has within it a fortune-telling ritual concerning marriage. The eve of Hambardzum has been described as a time when the universe seems to stop: a time when the heavens draw close to the earth, the stars exchange kisses, and the trees greet one another, an uncertain time that seems well-disposed for fortune telling.

Meuron. Holy oil or Chrism of the Armenian Apostolic Church. It is composed mostly of olive oil and forty-four other ingredients, including the oils of flowers. Meuron is used for the Confirmation Sacrament in which a baptized child receives the Holy Spirit. All Armenians who have been baptized in the apostolic faith have been anointed with a portion of the meuron that was originally prepared during the time of Saint Gregory the Illuminator. The Confirmation Sacrament in effect anoints or seals in the baptized individual with God. The Catholicos combines a new mixture of meuron every seven years using a portion from the previous blend. Before Christianity, meuron was reserved only to anoint the enthroning of royalty and for very special events. In later years it was used with extreme unction to heal the sick and to anoint the ordained clergy. Currently, meuron is also utilized to confirm a person's baptism and is distributed to all Armenian churches throughout the world.

ACKNOWLEDGEMENTS

The following people encouraged me in so many ways while I was writing this book and imparted valuable information: Ara Ghazarians, curator of the Armenian Cultural Foundation (Arlington, MA); my cousin Alice Markarian (midwife, Baghdad, Iraq); my brother Arthur Minas Sarkisian and his invaluable research; my aunt Rebecca Yeranian, who knew the stories; Armen Aroyan, who took me to the village of Keramet in 2009; Dikran Yepremian, my Armenian language teacher, who is also fluent in Turkish; my sister Lucille Sarkisian, who remembered more stories; Dikran Hacyan of the Armenian Cultural Association in Nice, France; Elise Antreassian of the Department of Youth and Education (Diocese of the Armenian Church of America–Eastern); Shahaniki Baharyan, keeper of family history; Barbara Merguerian, scholar and historian. I am indebted to my graphic designer, photographer, and editor, Valerie Turpen. Words cannot express my appreciation to Florence Pashayan for her support and help in providing invaluable information that added so much to the story of her mother, Aghavni, my father, Deli Sarkis, and the villagers of Keramet. Our friendship has lasted twenty-three years and counting. And to my husband, Glen E. Chesnut, for taking on someone forty-two years ago with a "lot of baggage," namely the Armenian genocide, and remaining my steadfast and supportive friend. Thank you, Glen, and all who helped bring this project to fruition.

SOURCES

Akcam, Taner. 2006. *A Shameful Act: The Armenian Genocide and the Question of Turkish Responsibility*. New York: Holt Paperbacks.

Balakian, Grigoris. 2009. *Armenian Golgotha: A Memoir of the Armenian Genocide, 1915–1918*. Translated by Peter Balakian with Aris Sevag. New York: Alfred A. Knopf.

Balsan, Francois. 1942 and 1945. *Les Surprises Du Kurdistan*, Paris. Edition J. Susse.

Bardakjian, K. B. 1985. *Hitler and the Armenian Genocide*. Cambridge, MA: Zoryan Institute.

Brandt, George. 1938. "Modern Magic Carpet to Bagdad." *The Seven Seas* (Autumn): 10-11, 22. Published by Hamburg-American Line. North German Lloyd. NYC.

Cetin, Fethiye. 2008. *My Grandmother*. Translated by Maureen Freely. London and New York: Verso.

Dadrian, Vahakn N. 1995. *The History of the Armenian Genocide*. Providence, RI: Berghahn Books.

Davis, Leslie A. 1989. *The Slaughterhouse Province: An American Diplomat's Report on the Armenian Genocide 1915–1917*. Edited by Susan K. Blair. New Rochelle, NY: Aristide D. Caratzas, Publisher.

Derogy, Jacques. 1990. *Resistance and Revenge: The Armenian Assassination of the Turkish Leaders Responsible for the 1915 Massacres and Deportations*. Translated by A. M. Berrett. New Brunswick, NJ: Transaction Publishers.

Dobkin, Marjorie Housepian. 1988. Smyrna 1922: *The Destruction of a City*. Kent, OH and London: Kent State University Press.

Lang, David Marshall. 1988. *The Armenians: A People in Exile*. London: Unwin Paperbacks.

Milton, Giles. 2008. *Paradise Lost: Smyrna 1922*. New York: Basic Books/Perseus Books Group.

Nalbandian, Inga. 2007. *Your Brother's Blood Cries Out.* Translated and edited by Victoria Rowe. London: Gomidas Institute.

Nigogossian, Hagop. *Memoirs of my Exile 1915–1929*, Bois Colombes, France, signed on January 6, 1958.

Papazian, Garabed Nigogos. *Statistics of Keramet Village.* Compiled and completed in 1966, Bourgas, Bulgaria.

Sarkisian, Sarkis Deli. He recounted his memoirs verbally while Ellen Sarkisian Chesnut wrote down his words. Transcribed from 1988–1995. All writings approved and signed by Deli Sarkis in 1995.

Taft, Elise Hagopian. 1981. *Rebirth: The Story of an Armenian Girl Who Survived the Genocide and Found Rebirth in America.* Plandome, NY: New Age Publishers.

Ungor, Ugur Umit. 2011. *Confiscation and Destruction: The Young Turk Seizure of Armenian Property.* Co-written with Mehmet Polatel. London: Continuum.

Uregian, Hovakim. 1982. "Smyrna Diary 1922, Memories of an Armenian Eyewitness from Two Unpublished Eyewitness Accounts of the Holocaust of Smyrna, September 1922." *The Armenian Review, Volume 35, No. 4–140* (Winter 1982).

A FAMOUS KERAMETSI

Archbishop Khoren Ashekian
Patriarch of the Armenians in Constantinople
(1888–1894)

Archbishop Khoren Ashekian was born in Keramet in 1842 was
ordained priest in 1863, and was later made a bishop in Holy
Etchmiadzin in 1871 at age 32. He became the dean of the Armash
Monastery the following year. He was an educator who edited the
periodical *Hooys*. He wrote the textbook *The Essence of Logic* and
translated a number of other books into Armenian. He opened
a grade school in Armash in 1872, naming it Ghevondiants, and
created the special curriculum.

While in Armash, the bishop was able to order and bring printing
equipment to Armash for the first time from Europe, thus
expanding its publishing capabilities. The Ghevondiants school
existed for nineteen years until the building was destroyed by fire
in 1888.

The archbishop was elected patriarch of Constantinople in 1888,
and the next year, upon the recommendation of Bishop Maghakia
Ormanian, he endorsed the opening of the famous Seminary of
Armash in 1889, giving his special *Encyclical of the Establishment*.
The seminary lasted twenty-five years and offered the Armenian
Church most worthy priests until its brutal closure by the Ottoman
Turks during WWI.

Patriarch Ashekian resigned from the office of the patriarch in
1894 and passed away in 1899.

ELLEN SARKISIAN CHESNUT

Born in Mosul, Iraq, in 1939, Ellen Sarkisian Chesnut came to the United States with her parents and baby brother on the *MS Boschfontein*, arriving in San Francisco on August 16, 1941. With a love of Armenian history and culture, her nonfiction articles *Wonder Woman, Kuzoom Park, Churpoteek, and Cousin Arsen* have been published in *ARARAT Quarterly*, a publication that encourages Armenian-American writers and artists.

Chesnut has received awards for her paintings and prints, which combine memory and myth. They have been featured in one-woman shows and have appeared in group exhibitions. Many of her works are in private collections. In 1995, Chesnut received the Visual Art High School Teacher Award through the San Francisco Unified School District. She retired from teaching in 2006 and lives with her husband in Northern California.

Ellen Sarkisian Chesnut in 1973 holding her drawing that was used for her woodcut, "Stories My Father Told Me."